MW00698037

Library of Congress Cataloging-in-Publication Data has been applied for.
Mastering Core SAT Words by William H. Shin

ISBN: 978-1-938462-15-3 (print) | ISBN: 978-1-938462-16-0 (eBook)

Published by Old Stone Press
Louisville, Kentucky 40207
First Edition, 2012
Printed in the United States of America

" *This is one of the most effective books for those who are preparing for the SAT. I noticed that all the words from the book had appeared on the SAT often. It is well organized by categories and made it easy to understand words that I had been having trouble with. I strongly recommend this book to students to study for the SAT Critical Reading and Writing exams.* **"**

Han Sol Kim *(James Caldwell High School)*
Admitted to State University of New York (SUNY),
Pre-Medicine

"

Mr. Shin has been my writing teacher for almost a year. If I were to study for the SAT by myself, or with a tutor, I would use Mr. Shin's book, Mastering Core SAT Words. *His book is different from other publishers' because he includes words that were used in the past SATs. Also, since it is current, it is updated with new vocabulary words many people may not be familiar with. So if you are a student who is studying for the SATs, or just looking for handy word books to study from, I strongly recommend* Mastering Core SAT Words!

"

Soojin Cho *(Ridgefield Memorial High School)*

MASTERING CORE
SAT WORDS

Ⓦ William H. Shin

This book contains as many as 1,395 core SAT words along with synonyms, definitions, and example sentences. In addition, in order to help students preparing for the SAT to memorize the words more effectively, certain words have stars (*), which indicate the degrees of difficulty of memorizing them. Based on my long-term SAT teaching degree experience, students preparing for the SAT must precisely learn the long-term definitions of the SAT words in this book to enhance their SAT Critical Reading scores, particularly on the sentence completion and the short reading passage sections. Once students have memorized all the words, they will be able to start dealing with questions related to the long passages more easily and efficiently. I have no single doubt that this book will enable students to become better SAT test takers.

I have been working as an SAT Critical Reading and Writing lecturer for more than fourteen years in both New York and New Jersey. In addition, I have made a ceaseless and indefatigable effort to analyze SAT Reasoning questions on a daily basis in order to become a better SAT lecturer and to meet my students' demands as well. Ultimately, it enabled me to start and complete this book. I am certain that this book will play a tremendously positive role in helping students boost their SAT Critical Reading scores.

I will always be grateful to my former and current SAT students, colleagues, and pianist, Lynn. Particularly, I would like to express my gratitude to Nashel and Hoon. Nashel spent numerous hours editing it; Hoon designed the cover. Without their help, I would not be able to publish it. I would like to dedicate *Mastering Core SAT Words* to them.

1. **Imperious** [im-**peer**-ee-uhs]
   adj syn: self-assured; domineering; overbearing.
   The *imperious* Queen demanded that her servants do back flips
   every time they came to her presence.

2. **Inscrutable** [in-**skroo**-tuh-buhl]
   adj def: hard to understand completely. (***)
   The judge's face was *inscrutable* as he read the juror's verdict,
   giving no clue as to what the verdict would be.

3. **Convivial** [kuhn-**viv**-ee-uhl]
   adj syn: lively; festive. (a convivial atmosphere)
   Jason always enjoys placing himself in a *convivial* environment.

4. **Solicitous** [suh-**lis**-i-tuhs]
   adj syn: concerned; attentive; eager. (**)
   The *solicitous* waitress stood next to the celebrity throughout
   the meal, ready to serve her.

5. **Emphasize** [**em**-fuh-sahyz]
   verb syn: underscore; focus.
   Tony tried to *emphasize* his main idea in the introduction of
   his essay.

6. **Histrionic** [his-tree-**oh**-ik]
   adj syn: of behavior, theatrical; dramatic. (*)
   def: behavior designed to impress. adv: histrionically.
   It is believed that European life is *histrionic* and dramatized.

7. **Ardor** [**ahr**-der]
   noun def: a strong feeling of passion, energy, or zeal. adj: ardent.
   The young revolutionary proclaimed his conviction with an *ardor*
   that excited the crowd.

8. **Limp** [limp]
   verb def: to walk with difficulty, without energy or will, easily bent. (**)
   The injury on his right leg left him *limping* for months.

9. **Halt** [hawlt]
   noun def: a stop, a temporary stoppage on a journey,
   or walk hesitatingly (**)
   Verb def: to make a stop.
   They *halted* operation during contract negotiation.
   The protest was at a *halt* when the police arrived.

10. **Robust** [**roh**-buhst]
   adj syn: strong and healthy; hardy.
   Many of those around her fell sick, but Esther was *robust* and
   sustained healthy throughout the flu epidemic.

11. **Prompt** [prompt]
   verb def: acting with alacrity; ready, made quickly and immediately.
   What *prompted* you to come to the art convention?
   My interest in sculptures *prompted* me to come.

12. **Facile** [**fas**-il]
   adj syn: easy; unconstrained. (**)
   The one-minute political commercial favors a candidate with *facile*
   opinions rather than serious, thoughtful solutions.

13. **Phenomenal** [fi-**na**--ma-nl]
   adj syn: remarkable; exceeding; extraordinary.
   Michael Jordan is the most *phenomenonal* basketball player in the
   history of NBA in the United States.

14. **Subsequent** [**suhb**-si-kwuhnt]
   adj def: following a specific event.
   Subsequent to their move to Chicago, Mary and James bought a
   new car along with a nice apartment.

15. **Undermine** [uhn-der-**mahyn**]
   verb syn: to sabotage; thwart. (**)
   John made a ceaseless effort to *undermine* Emily's
   academic achievement.

16. **Debacle** [dey-**bah**-kuhl]
    noun def: an utter defeat or failure; a sudden collapse or downfall.
    A strong and wealthy government can afford a military *debacle*.

17. **Dissolve** [dih-**zolv**]
    verb def: make or become liquid. syn: disappear. (**)
    It is a fact that sugar *dissolves* quicker in hot water than
    in cold water.

18. **Reinforce** [ree-in-**fawrs**]
    verb syn: to strengthen; to support.
    Lynn continuously *reinforces* her unique piano techniques by
    practicing everyday.

19. **Thwart** [thwawrt]
    verb def: to prevent or to stop from happening; to frustrate (****)
    Thwarted in its attempt to get the food out of the plastic box, the
    chimp threw the box to the ground in frustration.

20. **Forfeit** [**fawr**-fit]
    noun def: a penalty for a breach of contract or neglect; a fine. (**)
    If SAT test takers fail to take the test on a designated date, there is a
    forfeit in the form of a test fee from the College Board.

21. **Redoubtable** [ri-**dou**-tuhl-buhl]
    adj syn: inspiring respect; awe; fear. (***)
    Johnson's knowledge, experience, and personal clout made him
    a *redoubtable* political opponent.

22. **Toady** [**toh**-dee]
    noun syn: fawner hanger-on; yes-man; sycophant. (**)
    Most of the office workers hate the office *toady*, who spends most
    of his time complimenting the boss.

23. **Harangue** [huh-**rang**]
    noun def: a lengthy speech or lecture.
    Tonia delivered a long *harangue* about poor customer service
    he received from the restaurant he visited last week.

24. **Temperance** [**tem**-per-uhns]
     noun def: moderation or restrain in feeling and behavior. (***)
     The majority of professional athletes practice *temperance* in their personal habits; they know that too much eating or drinking can damage their performance.

25. **Conciliatory** [kuhn-**sil**-ee-uh-taw-ee]
     adj syn: seeking agreement; compromise; reconciliation.
     As a *conciliatory* gesture, the union members unanimously agreed to postpone the strike and to continue negotiations with the management.

26. **Indulge** [in-**duhlj**]
     verb def: to give in to a craving or desire. syn: self-indulgence.
     Steve *indulged* himself with a weekend at a luxurious spa.

27. **Appease** [uh-**peez**]
     verb syn: to satisfy; placate; calm; pacify.
     To *appease* the bawling infants, we sang a variety of lullabies.

28. **Affluent** [**af**-loo-uhnt]
     adj syn: rich; abundant; bounty; abound. (**)
     Lynda, an *affluent* woman, donated a large sum of money to charity.

29. **Lavish** [**lav**-ish]
     adj syn: liberal; wasteful. (*)
     The Prince's *lavish* gifts pleased John Hancock.

30. **Acute** [uh-**kyoot**]
     adj syn: sharp; pointed severe.
     There is an *acute* shortage of food supply in the city, and people will starve if food is not supplied soon.

31. **Corpulence** [**kawr**-pyuh-luhns]
     noun syn: obesity; fatness; bulkiness. (***)
     Alice's *corpulence* increased as she spent several hours everyday eating and drinking.

32. Vex [veks]
    verb syn: to irritate; annoy; trouble. (**)
        Fermat's last theorem was one of the most famous, and
        most *vexing* of all mathematical enigmas.

33. Ailment [eyl-muhnt]
    noun syn: illness; a minor and chronicle disease. (*)
        Crystal's ongoing smoking habit turned out to be one of her
        unavoidable *ailments*.

34. Succulent [suhk-**yuh**-luhnt]
    adj syn: juicy; full of vitality; freshness. (***)
        The famished student deliciously enjoyed the *succulent* porterhouse
        steak with a variety of relish.

35. Redolent [**red**-l-uhnt]
    adj syn: fragrant; having a strong smell.
        The *redolent* smell emitting from the kitchen reminded Eric of
        his childhood.

36. Cerebral [suh-**ree**-bruhl]
    adj def: of brain; intellectual rather than emotional. (**)
        Lisa's habit of disregarding people's thoughts made her a *cerebral*
        person rather than a sympathetic one.

37. Amiable [ey-mee-uh-buhl]
    adj syn: likable; agreeable; friendly.
        Alex was an *amiable* lab partner, always smiling, on time, and
        ready to work.

38. Autocrat [**aw**-tuh-krat]
    noun syn: tyrant; dictator.
        Hitler is the most infamous *autocrat* in history.

39. Deface [dih-feys]
verb syn: to mar the appearance; vandalize. (***)
> After the wall was torn down, the statues of the Communist leaders were *defaced* all over the former Eastern block.

40. Connoisseur [kon-uh-sur]
noun def: a person with a refined taste.
> The wine was finally released to the market after a *connoisseur* had checked the quality of the wine.

41. Inebriate [in-ee-bree-eyt]
verb syn: to make drunk; intoxicate. (**)
> Obviously *inebriated,* the best man slurred his words during his speech at the wedding.

42. Adulation [aj-uh-ley-shuhn]
noun syn: high praise; flatter; toady. (***)
> After Lynn's piano recital, the audience lavished her with *adulation.*

43. Speculation [spek-yuh-ley-shuhn]
noun def: contemplation. (**)
> If you want to ensure that you have a nest egg to retire on, you should not engage in too much wild financial *speculation.*

44. Callous [kal-uhs]
adj syn: thick-skinned; insensitive. (***)
> Dr. Rubinstein *callously* ignored the pathetic whining of the injured puppy.

45. Arable [ar-uh-buhl]
adj def: fit for growing crops. (*)
> The first settlers wrote glowing reports about the New World, praising its vast acres of *arable* land ready for the plow.

❝ *The best way to learn vocabulary is through extensive and varied reading. But students preparing for examinations such as the SAT —even if they are avid readers—often need a review of the lexical items that reappear in academic literature, especially if they are preparing for entrance examinations. These words tend to reappear in college entrance examinations and are indispensable if students are to make sense not only of academic reading but also the kinds of items found on standardized tests. William Shin's book* Mastering Core SAT Words *is ideal for students looking to review core vocabulary.*

The chapters are concise, the word lists manageable for someone working in self-study. Shin's definitions are to the point and his examples help to clarify word meanings. He often uses appositives, for example, to help students see the meaning of the word. Words are asterisked to help students identify those words that pose more difficulty.

Shin has many years' experience working with students to prepare them for standardized examinations—and it shows in this book. There are exercises for students to complete and—while I wish they were more varied—they do focus the student on the word to be mastered. This book is a very helpful study guide for students looking to review and reinforce core college level vocabulary. **❞**

Anthony DeFazio
*Multilingual/Multicultural Studies, New York University
Former teacher, International High School, New York City.*

Synonym

1. Inscrutable
    A) Halt
    B) Sequent
    C) Robust
    D) Undermine
    E) Difficult to understand

2. Ardor
    A) Dissolve
    B) Toady
    C) Harangue
    D) Zeal
    E) Subsequent

3. Toady
    A) Indulge
    B) Vex
    C) Acute
    D) Flatter
    E) Corpulence

4. Lavish
    A) Ailment
    B) Deface
    C) Wasteful
    D) Amiable
    E) Cerebral

5. Succulent
    A) Juicy
    B) Vandalize
    C) Inebriate
    D) Contemplation
    E) Insensitive

6. Thwart
   A) Moderate
   B) Disappear
   C) Toady
   D) Prevent
   E) Harangue

7. Indulge
   A) Corpulence
   B) Lavish
   C) Craving
   D) Reinforce
   E) Redoubtable

8. Indignant
   A) Remission
   B) Incense
   C) Abash
   D) Vicarious
   E) Erratic

Answer keys

1) E   2) D   3) D   4) C   5) A   6) D   7) C   8) B

Antonym

1. Emphasize
 A) Ardent
 B) Overbearing
 C) Festive
 D) Undermine
 E) Convivial

2. Undermine
 A) Forfeit
 B) Sycophant
 C) Restrain
 D) Strengthen
 E) Temperance

3. Appease
 A) Allay
 B) Lessen
 C) Aggravate
 D) Severe
 E) Bounty

4. Vex
 A) Soothe
 B) Acute
 C) Abrade
 D) Agitate
 E) Nettle

5. Conciliatory
 A) Assuaging
 B) Mollifying
 C) Antagonistic
 D) Placate
 E) Severe

6. Cerebral
- A) Emotional
- B) Erudite
- C) Recondite
- D) Agreeable
- E) Vitality

7. Callous
- A) Impassive
- B) Stubborn
- C) Unaffected
- D) Compassionate
- E) Arable

8. Undermine
- A) Agonize
- B) Strengthen
- C) Vindicate
- D) Insolence
- E) Disdain

9. Redolent
- A) Noisome
- B) Sophistry
- C) Tonal
- D) Munificent
- E) Erudite

Answer Keys

1) D   2) D   3) C   4) A   5) C   6) A   7) D   8) B   9) A

1. **Apprehension** [ap-ri-**hen**-shuhn]
   noun syn: fear; discernment; capture. (**)
   > The tourists refused to drive their rental cars through downtown Chicago because they felt an *apprehension* that they might get carjacked.

2. **Viscous** [**vis**-kuhs]
   adj def: thick; syrupy; sticky.
   > The *viscous* sap trickled slowly down the trunk of the tree.

3. **Articulate** [arh-**tik**-yuh-lit]
   adj def: well spoken, lucidly presented. (**)
   > Alex's *articulate* argument was so persuasive that most of the students in class agreed with him.

4. **Spontaneous** [spon-**tey**-nee-uhs]
   adj def: happening without plan or outside cause.
   > When the news of Kennedy's assassination broke, people everywhere gathered in a *spontaneous* effort to share their shock and grief.
   > Scrooge's act of kindness was *spontaneous* and unexpected.

5. **Profound** [pruh-**found**]
   adj syn: deep; wise; sagacious.
   > Both the Book of Ecclesiastes and the Tao Te Chin contain *profound* observation about human life.

6. **Reprehensible** [rep-ri-**hen**-suh-buhl]
   adj syn: deserving criticism; censure. (***)
   > Not all fans agree that he deserves to be excluded from the Baseball Hall of Fame, although the athlete's misdeed was *reprehensible*.

7. **Palliate** [**pal**-ee-yet]
   verb syn: to make less serious; ease. (*)
   > The crime was so vicious that the defense lawyer could not *palliate* it for the jury.

8. **Depreciate** [dih-**pree**-shee-yet]
   verb syn: to lose value; devalue. ant: appreciate.
   Erica sold her house in fear that its value would *depreciate* due to the nuclear reactor being built around the corner.

9. **Litigation** [lit-i-**gey**-shuhn]
   noun syn: lawsuit.
   Jenny finally won her court case after years of *litigation*.

10. **Compendious** [kuhm-**pen**-dee-uhs]
    adj def: comprehensive but fairly brief. (**)
    Kelly's *compendious* argument helped her students to grasp the underlying concept of the Theory of Relativity effectively.

11. **Swindle** [**swin**-dl]
    verb def: to cheat a person of money or possession. (***)
    Sophie had the bad habit of *swindling* her friend's allowance.

12. **Gullible** [**guhl**-uh-buhl]
    adj syn: easily fooled or deceived. (**)
    When the sweepstakes entry form arrived bearing the message, *"You May be a winner!"* my *gullible* neighbor tried to claim a prize.

13. **Allay** [uh-**ley**]
    verb syn: to lessen; ease; soothe.
    The nurse attempted to *allay* the couple's fear that their son's health had deteriorated.

14. **Prey** [prey]
    noun def: an animal that is hunted or killed by another for food.
    A hungry predator came out of its den to seek its *prey*.

15. **Necromancy** [**nek**-ruh-man-see]
    noun def: black magic.
    Her grandmother was accused of witchcraft and *necromancy*.

16. Perishable [per-i-shuh-buhl]
adj syn: ruinable; subject to destruction.
Steve always forgets to put *perishable* vegetables into the fridge.

17. Dearth [durth]
noun syn: lack; scarcity; insufficient. (**)
The *dearth* of supply in our town made it difficult to hold out
for long against the attack from the enemy.

18. Inevitable [in-ev-i-tuh-buhl]
adj def: unable to be avoided. (***)
When the Japanese attacked Pearl Harbor, American involvement
in World War II was *inevitable*.

19. Discordant [dis-kawr-dnt]
adj syn: harsh-sounding; badly out of tune.
The violin sounded completely *discordant* after not having been
played for 50 years.

20. Legendary [lej-uhn-der-ee]
adj def: celebrated or described in legend; a legend hero.
Hank Aaron has been considered as a *legendary* professional
baseball player.

21. Redundancy [ri-duhn-duhn-see]
noun def: unnecessary repetition.
Let's delete a few paragraphs to remove the *redundancy* in
this section of the book.

22. Somber [som-ber]
adj syn: dark; gloomy; melancholy; dismal. (**)
Everyone at the funeral was wearing dark, *somber* clothes
except for the little in girl in the flowered dress.

23. Wistful [wist-fuhl]
adj def: characterized by melancholy, longing, or yearning. (***)
The car accident caused by the reckless taxi driver put the family
in a *wistful* mood.

24. Penetrate [pen-i-treyt]
verb def: to pierce or pass into or through. (*)
The fog lights *penetrated* the mist.

25. Brevity [brev-i-tee]
noun def: shortness of time or duration; briefness; terseness.
Brevity is the soul of wit.
There was a *brevity* in her presentation because she was late for
her next meeting.

26. Rigid [ri-jed]
adj syn: firmly fixed; inflexible; strict; severe.
The boarding school always sticks to *rigid* rules that keep
the students under absolute control.

27. Florid [flawr-id]
adj syn: gaudy; showy; extremely ornate; ruddy; flushed. (**)
The palace had been decorated in an excessively *florid* style; every
surface had been carved and gilded.

28. Opaque [oh-peyk]
adj def: impervious to light; difficult to understand. (*)
The heavy buildup of dirt and grime on the windows almost
made them *opaque*.

29. Irrepressible [ir-i-pres-uh-buhl]
adj def: incapable of being repressed or restrained.
Her laughter was *irrepressible* to his hilarious joke.

30. Negligible [neg-li-juh-buhl]
adj def: not worth considering. syn: trifle; trivial. (***)
It is obvious from our *negligible* dropout rate that our students love
our program.

31. Magnanimous [mag-nan-uh-muhs]
adj syn: generous. def: noble in spirit.
Although at first he seemed mean, Uncle Frank turned out to
be a very *magnanimous* man.

32. Erratic [ih-**rat**-ik]

adj def: deviating from the usual or proper course in
   conduct opinion (***)
   syn: eccentric; queer; erratic behavior.
   Eric's *erratic* behavior caused Jane to break up with him.

33. Idiosyncrasy [id-ee-uh-**sing**-kruh-see]

noun syn: peculiarity of temperament; eccentricity.
   His numerous *idiosyncrasies* included a fondness for wearing bright
   green shoes with mauve socks.

34. Regress [ri-**gres**]

verb def: to move back; revert to an earlier form or state. (**)
   Elderly people who suffer from senility often *regress* to
   the early years of their childhood.

35. Moderate [**mod**-rit]

adj syn: reasonable; not extreme.
   "Please make sure my dish is *moderately* spiced; I like a little
   spice, but not too much," the customer instructed the waiter.

36. Catastrophe [kuh-**tas**-truh-fee]

noun def: disastrous event. syn: disaster; ruin; devastation. (***)
   The eruption was truly a *catastrophe*; lava and ash buried several
   towns on the slopes of the volcano.

37. Devoid [dih-**void**]

adj def: totally lacking. (**)
   Esther is really *devoid* of tact; did you hear her tell that off-color
   joke at the funeral?

38. Disparage [dih-**spar**-ij]

verb syn: to belittle, speak disrespectfully about. (***)
   Brian tried to *disparage* his brother's dancing skills by pointing
   out every mistake he made on the floor.

39. Procrastinate [proh-**kras**-tuh-neyt]
verb def: to put off; to delay. (**)
Students tend to *procrastinate* on their homework until the night before it is due.

40. Meddler [**med**-lr]
noun def: person interfering in other's affairs.
Mike is a real *meddler*, always sticking his nose in places it does not belong.

41. Scoff [skawf]
verb syn: to deride; ridicule; sneer.
The baby *scoffed* at the notion that cows could jump over the moon; he was too smart to believe that.

42. Intrude [in-**trood**]
verb def: to thrust or bring in without invitation or permission.
Hitler *intruded* Austria without prior notice in 1936.

43. Dispense [**dis**-spans]
verb syn: to distribute; administer. (*)
Pharmacists will only *dispense* medicine to customers with doctors' prescriptions.

44. Vacuous [**vak**-yoo-uhs]
adj syn: empty-headed; not serious.
The book that William loved when he was seven struck him utterly *vacuous* when he was twenty-five, but he still liked the pictures.

45. Infelicitous [in-ful-**lis**-thus]
adj def: the quality or state of being unhappy. (***)
syn: misfortune; inapt.
Melissa has been facing *infelicitous* situations for the past three weeks.

Synonym

1. Apprehension
    A) Anxiety
    B) Calmness
    C) Trepidation
    D) Sagacious
    E) Criticism

2. Reprehensible
    A) Respectable
    B) Discernment
    C) Accuse
    D) Censure
    E) Palliate

3. Profound
    A) Ignorant
    B) Soothe
    C) Deep
    D) Appreciate
    E) Swindle

4. Depreciate
    A) Overrate
    B) Devalue
    C) Deceive
    D) Lessen
    E) Litigation

5. Perishable
- A) Endurance
- B) Decaying
- C) Dismal
- D) Yearning
- E) Celebrate

6. Discordant
- A) Conflicting
- B) Concordant
- C) Avoid
- D) Decay
- E) Melancholy

7. Somber
- A) Cheerful
- B) Joyous
- C) Gloomy
- D) Harsh
- E) Perishable

8. Viscous
- A) Furious
- B) Subterfuge
- C) Sedulous
- D) Meticulous
- E) Sticky

Answer Keys

1)A 2) D 3)C 4) B 5) B 6) A 7) C 8) E

Antonym

1. Inevitable
   A) Determined
   B) Doomed
   C) Avoidable
   D) Ordained
   E) Legendary

2. Wistful
   A) Contemplate
   B) Nostalgic
   C) Reflective
   D) Uncaring
   E) Repetition

3. Florid
   A) Gaudy
   B) Plain
   C) Showy
   D) Garnish
   E) Rhetorical

4. Opaque
   A) Darkened
   B) Turbid
   C) Dull
   D) Terse
   E) Lucid

5. Negligible
   A) Important
   B) Inconsequential
   C) Trivial
   D) Strict
   E) Ornate

6. Dearth
>A) Scarcity
>B) Abundance
>C) Privation
>D) Deficiency
>E) Decay

7. Disparage
>A) Belittle
>B) Vilify
>C) Approve
>D) Devastation
>E) Peculiarity

8. Redundancy
>A) Entangle
>B) Vulgar
>C) Compulsive
>D) Tonal
>E) Necessary

9. Procrastinate
>A) Futile
>B) Quicken
>C) Castigate
>D) Exalt
>E) Inception

Answer Keys

1) C 2) D 3) B 4) E 5) A 6) B 7) C 8) E 9) B

1. **Vivacious** [vi-**vey**-shuhs]-
   adj syn: lively; spirited
   > Jan was extremely *vivacious* and outgoing; she was always ready to try something new.

2. **Futile** [**fyoo**-tahyhl]
   adj syn: ineffective; useless; unimportant; pointless. (**)
   > My attempt to reach the shore before the storm was *futile*; the wind blew me back into the middle of the lake.

3. **Boor** [boor]
   noun def: crude person, one lacking manners or taste.
   > "That utter *boor* ruined my recital with his constant guffawing!" wailed the pianist.

4. **Integrity** [in-**teg**-ri-tee]
   noun syn: decency; honesty; wholeness.
   > The candidate's *integrity* made him a refreshing contrast to his sleazy political opponents.

5. **Whimsical** [**hwim**-zi-kuhl]
   adj def: playful or fanciful idea. (**)
   > The ballet was *whimsical*, delighting the children with its imaginative characters and unpredictable sets.

6. **Sedulous** [**sej**-uh-luhs]
   adj syn: diligent; preserving; assiduous. (****)
   > Josh always shows a *sedulous* attitude toward the classes he takes in college.

7. **Vindictive** [vin-**dik**-tiv]
   adj syn: spiteful; vengeful; unforgiving. (***)
   > After her husband left her for a young model, the *vindictive* ex-wife decided to destroy their relationship.

" *This is the best mnemonic vocabulary book I've come across. Most vocabulary books expect the reader to simply memorize dozens of words from a definition, an etymology; however, this book contains core SAT words along with synonyms, definitions and examples. Using this book will quickly and thoroughly prepare you for the SAT Critical Reading test. The gripes I have do not take away from the quality of this excellent book and the effectiveness of the methods. I can't wait to read the next volume as well! Definitely buy this book NOW, you will not regret it!* "

SUNGHO YOON, Ph.D., A.M.ASCE
Research Professor
Polytechnic Institute of New York University

" *This book contains numerous vocabulary words that are often on the SATs. Before I had read this book, my vocabulary wasn't my strongest SAT skill. However, after reading the core vocabulary words that were presented in this book (and also by solving the problems inside) my vocabulary became one of my strengths. This book contains every single word that has been used by the SAT test makers and is designed to bolster your skills in the Critical Reading sentence completion section. I have also learned many things in the research paper that was written by Mr. Shin and learned numerous things about the SAT and each of its sections. I am taking the SAT from Mr. Shin's research paper in June 2012 and am confident that I will answer all of the sentence completion questions correctly. Thank You, Mr. Shin.* "

Daniel Hong *(Fort Lee High School)*

8. **Petulance** [**pech**-uh-luhns]
   noun syn: rudeness; peevishness. (**)
   > The student's *petulance* annoyed the teacher who liked her young students to be cheerful and cooperative.

9. **Prosaic** [proh-**zey**-ik]
   adj syn: everyday; ordinary; dull.
   > "Paul's Case" tells the story of a boy who longs to escape from the *prosaic* life of a clerk into a world of wealth, glamour, and beauty.

10. **Cursory** [**kur**-suh-ree]
    adj syn: hastily done; superficial.
    > The copy editor gave the article a *cursory* look, missing dozens of errors.

11. **Exonerate** [ig-**zon**-uh-reyt]
    verb def: to free from blame. (**)
    > Although John was suspected at first of being involved in the bombing, later evidence fortunately *exonerated* him.

12. **Flaunt** [flawnt]
    verb syn: to show off; boast; pompous. (*)
    > Jeffrey *flaunted* his engagement ring to everyone at the office.

13. **Reluctance** [ri-**luhk**-tuh-hs]
    noun syn: unwillingness; disinclination.
    > The president used to have a strong *reluctance* to speak in public.

14. **Gratitude** [**grat**-i-tood]
    noun def: the quality or feeling of being grateful or thankful.
    > He expressed his *gratitude* to everyone on the staff.

15. **Reign** [reyn]
    verb def: to possess or to exercise sovereign power or authority.
    > King George had *reigned* his country until the day he passed away.

16. Demean [dih-meen]
verb syn: to degrade; humiliate; humble. (**)

The editor felt that it would *demean* the newspaper to publish letters containing obscenities.

17. Opprobrious [uh-proh-bree-uhs]
adj syn: disgraceful; contemptuous.

In spite of his *opprobrious* addiction to gambling, the governor was re-elected once again.

18. Chagrin [shuh-grin]
noun syn: shame; embarrassment; humiliation. (**)

It is no doubt that the director felt an excellent deal of *chagrin* after vomiting on his neighbor at the company banquet.

19. Hail [heyl]
verb syn: to cheer; salute; greet; welcome; to acclaim; approve. (***)

Many people *hailed* the conquerors.

They *hailed* the recent advances in medicine.

20. Mutual [myoo-choo-uhl]
adj def: having the same relation each toward the other.

John and Alice established their *mutual* company.

21. Divert [di-vurt]
noun def: the act of diverting or turning aside, as from a course or purpose.

A channel was made to *divert* the flow of water from one course to another.

22. Disparity [dih-spar-i-tee]
noun def: difference in quality and kind. (*)

There is often a *disparity* between the kind of high quality television people say they want and the low-blow program they actually watch.

23. Indignant [in-**dig**-nuhnt]

adj syn: angry; incensed; offend. (**)

 The innocent passerby was *indignant* when the police treated him as a suspect in the crime.

24. Detach [dih-**tach**]

verb syn: to unfasten and separate; disengage; disunite.

 The company decided to *detach* Alex from a special mission.

25. Myriad [**mir**-ee-uhd]

noun syn: immense number; multitude. (***)

 Crystal moved to New York City to take advantage of the *myriad* of modeling opportunities available to her there.

26. Remission [ri-**mish**-uhn]

noun syn: lessening; relaxation. (**)

 Johnson was relieved to discover that her cancer had gone into *remission*.

27. Rebellion [ri-**bel**-yuhn]

noun def: organized, and armed resistance to one's government.

 The government made a tremendous effort to suppress the *rebellion*.

28. Fortify [**fawr**-tuh-fahy]

verb def: to strengthen or protect against attack; surround.

 Joan Arc re-built a wall to *fortify* the ability to protect her castle.

29. Foster [**faw**-ster]

verb syn: to nourish; cultivate; promote.

 The record agent *fostered* the development of his clients by sending them to singing lessons.

30. Quibble [**kwib**-uhl]

verb def: to argue about insignificant and irrelevant details. (***)

 Ignoring the widening crack in the dam, the engineers *quibbled* over whose turn it was to make coffee.

31. Ineffable [in-ef-uh-buhl]
adj def: difficult to describe or express. (***)
> Simon gazed in silence at the sunrise over the Taj Mahal with his eyes reflecting the *ineffable* sense of wonder.

32. Consummate [kon-shu-meyt]
verb syn: to complete; finish; perfect. (**)
> The deal was *consummated* with a handshake and the payment of the agreed-upon fee.

33. Sermon [sur-muhn]
noun def: a discourse for the purpose of religious instruction.
> June was deeply impressed by the *sermon* delivered by the rector.

34. Fidelity [fi-del-i-tee]
noun syn: loyalty.
> A traitor is someone whose *fidelity* is questioned.

35. Vacillate [vas-uh-leyt]
verb syn: to waver; to show indecision. (**)
> The customer held up the line as he *vacillated* between ordering chocolate chip or rocky road ice cream.

36. Steadfast [sted-fast]
adj def: fixed in direction; steadily directed resolution.
> Lynn and June have been long time *steadfast* friends.

37. Interpose [in-ter-pohz]
verb syn: to insert; to intervene.
> The policeman *interposed* himself between the two men who were about to start fighting.

38. Inkling [ingk-ling]
noun def: hint; vague idea. (**)
> They didn't give us an *inkling* of what was going to happen.

39. Polarize [poh-luh-rahz]

verb def: to separate into opposing groups or forces. (**)

For many years, the abortion debate *polarized* the American people, with many people voicing extreme views and a few trying to find a middle ground.

40. Vindicate [vin-di-keyt]

verb syn: to confirm; justify; defeat.

Lincoln's Gettysburg Address was intended to *vindicate* the objectives of the Union in the Civil War.

41. Censure [sen-sher]

verb syn: to blame; decry; condemn; criticize; rebuke. (***)

The news that the congressman had embarrassed several women brought *censure* from a number of people.

42. Discern [dis-surn]

verb def: to perceive something obscure.

It is easy to *discern* the difference between real butter and butter-flavored topping.

43. Holistic [hoh-lis-tik]

adj def: empathizing importance of the whole and interdependence of its part.

Eric is studying internal medicine and believes in a *holistic* approach to healing.

44. Animosity [an-uh-mos-i-tee]

noun syn: active enmity.

By advocating cuts in campaign spending and limits on congressional powers, the reform candidate seemed to invite the *animosity* of the party's leader.

45. Equanimity [ee-kwuh-nim-i-tee]

noun syn: calmness of temperance; composure; tranquility.

Even the inevitable strains of caring for an ailing mother did not disturb Bea's *equanimity*.

Alex Lee
Director of RECAS ACADEMY USA

Synonym

1. Futile
   A) Fruitful
   B) Placid
   C) Useless
   D) Abundant
   E) Scanty

2. Sedulous
   A) Assiduous
   B) Demean
   C) Enervate
   D) Circumspect
   E) Justify

3. Vindictive
   A) Forgiving
   B) Creed
   C) Argument
   D) Revengeful
   E) Acquire

4.Petulant
   A) Agile
   B) Malign
   C) Indulge
   D) Captious
   E) Parry

5. Cursory
- A) Meticulous
- B) Guffaw
- C) Charlatan
- D) Creed
- E) Hasty

6. Exonerate
- A) Accuse
- B) Condemn
- C) Excuse
- D) Vitality
- E) Treatise

7. Reluctance
- A) Averse
- B) Unwilling
- C) Revere
- D) Fragrant
- E) Pale

8. Discern
- A) Discriminate
- B) Overlook
- C) Nonchalant
- D) Exonerate
- E) Connive

Answer Keys

1) C 2) A 3) D 4) D 5) E 6) C 7) B 8) A

Antonym

1. Demean
- A) Humiliate
- B) Derogate
- C) Enhance
- D) Sedulous
- E) Abase

2. Chagrin
- A) Displeasure
- B) Delight
- C) Abash
- D) Fretfulness
- E) Liberate

3. Diversion
- A) Aberration
- B) Digression
- C) Timid
- D) Conforming
- E) Virtuous

4. Indignant
- A) Acrimonious
- B) Furious
- C) Plentiful
- D) Zenith
- E) Gleeful

5. Detach
- A) Attach
- B) Dismount
- C) Segregate
- D) Influx
- E) Fidelity

6. Foster
- A) Assist
- B) Discourage
- C) Sham
- D) Spate
- E) Tacit

7. Ineffable
- A) Celestial
- B) Pinnacle
- C) Describable
- D) Fiasco
- E) Dearth

8. Vindicate
- A) Forbade
- B) Absolve
- C) Subvert
- D) Accuse
- E) Fertilize

9. Animosity
- A) good-will
- B) Antagonism
- C) Eclectic
- D) Regress
- E) Debacle

Answer Keys

1) C 2) B 3) D 4) E 5) A 6) B 7) C 8) D 9) A

1. **Convolute** [**kon**-vah-loot]
   adj syn: twisting; complicate; intricate.
   Tax law has become so *convoluted* that it is easy for people to accidentally violate it.

2. **Somber** [**som**-ber]
   adj syn: gloomy; depressing; dark. (**)
   From the doctor's grim expression, I could tell he had *somber* news.

3. **Unsophisticated** [uhn-suh-**fis**-ti-key-tid]
   adj syn: simple; artless; pure; genuine.
   James' *unsophisticated* behaviors seemed to surprise his friends.

4. **Raconteur** [rak-uhn-**tur**]
   noun syn: witty, skillful storyteller
   The *raconteur* kept all the passengers entertained with his stories during the six-hour flight.

5. **Exasperation** [ig-zas-puh-**rey**-shuhn]
   noun syn: irritation. (***)
   The catcher could not hide his *exasperation* when the pitcher denied listening to his advice, throwing a series of pitches that resulted in homeruns for the opposing team.

6. **Inadequate** [in-**ad**-i-kwit]
   adj syn: not enough; short.
   The king frequently provided his people with an *inadequate* amount of food.

7. **Pendant** [**pen**-duhnt]
   noun def: hanging ornament.
   Tim wears a jade *pendant* inherited from his mother as a symbol of a filial piety.

8. **Ponderous** [**pon**-der-uhs]
   adj syn: weighty; heavy; large. (**)
   Sam carried a *ponderous* burden on his back.

9. **Plea** [plee]
   noun syn: an appeal or entreaty, an excuse; pretext.
   Tom begged on the *plea* that his car was not working and
   therefore, was late to the job interview.

10. **Unprecedented** [uhn-**pres**-i-den-tid]
    adj def: without previous instance; never before known.
    Alex had a plan to throw an *unprecedented* birthday party
    for his son.

11. **Warp** [wawrp]
    verb syn: bend or twist out of shape.
    Erica decided not to *warp* a U shape branch because it
    looked beautiful to her.

12. **Wag** [wag]
    verb def: to move from side to side, to shake at someone.
    When John entered into the house, a dog was staring at him,
    wagging its tail.

13. **Connive** [kuh-**nahyv**]
    verb def: to cooperate secretly; inspire. (**)
    They *connived* to take over the business.

14. **Concord** [**kon**-kawd]
    noun syn: agreement. (***)
    The manager and the employees were in *concord* over
    the necessity of improving the product.

15. **Contagious** [kuhn-**tey**-juhs]
    adj def: capable of being transmitted by bodily contact with an infected
    person or object.
    It is generally believed that mosquitoes spread various *contagious*
    diseases in the summer time.

16. Contempt [kuhn-tempt]
noun syn: vile, or worthless; disdain; scorn. (**)
> Sophie showed a profound *contempt* for Daniel's abnormal behavior.

17. Propensity [pruh-pen-si-tee]
noun syn: inclination; tendency.
> She has a *propensity* to lash out at others when under stress, so we leave her alone as much as possible.

18. Forestall [fohr-stawl]
verb syn: to prevent; hinder; stop (**)
> The government *forestalled* a riot by deploying police.

19. Momentous [moh-men-tuhs]
adj def: of great or far-reaching importance or consequence.
> Roger was unable to capitalize on the *momentous* opportunity.

20. Decisive [dih-sahy-siv]
adj def: having the power or quality of deciding; crucial. (**)
> The general was known for his *decisive* manner.

21. Constructive [kuhn-struhk-tiv]
adj def: helping to improve; promoting further.
> He always plays a significant role in providing his students with *constructive* criticism.

22. Cloak [klohk]
noun def: something that covers or conceals; disguise; pretense.
> Catherine arrived at the opera *cloaked* in green velvet.

23. Entangle [en-tang-guhl]
verb syn: to make tangle; ensnarl; intertwine. (***)
> Susan had been *entangled* by intrigue before she passed away.

24. Intermittent [in-ter-**mit**-tent]
adj def: starting and stopping. (**)
> The flow of traffic was *intermittent* on the highway, but the commuters were grateful that it had not stopped completely.

25. Dubious [**doo**-bee-uhs]
adj def: doubtful; questionable; uncertain.
> The soldier seemed to be involved in a *dubious* batter.

26. Extravagant [ik-**strav**-a-gant]
adj def: excessive or unnecessary expenditure or outlay. (*)
> June's *extravagant* shopping habit made everyone in the classroom speechless.

27. Bias [**bahy**-uhs]
noun syn: a particular tendency; inclination.
> Cindy usually prevents *biased* consideration of a question.

28. Pursue [per-**soo**]
verb syn: to carry on; continue (a course of action).
> Stanley decided to fly to Moscow to *pursue* higher education.

29. Humble [**huhm**-buhl]
adj def: the quality or condition of being humble; modest behavior.
> Jessica showed *humble* attitude towards her teacher in class.

30. Smugness [**smuhg**-nis]
noun syn: self-satisfied; superiority; correctness; complacent. (***)
> Angelina walked into the classroom with a sense of *smugness*.

31. Standoffish [stan-**aw**-fish]
adj def: somewhat aloof or deserved; cold and unfriendly
> Sarah has a strong tendency to be a bit *standoffish* with strangers.

32. Consolation [kon-suh-ley-shuhn]

noun def: relief or comfort in sorrow or suffering. (**)

Although we miss our dog very much, it is a *consolation* to know that she died quickly without suffering.

33. Blunt [bluhnt]

adj def: abrupt in address or manner, a blunt ill-time question.

His isolation has made him *blunt* about other people's feelings.

34. Phantom [**fan**-tuhm]

adj def: named, included, or recorded but nonexistence.

Payroll checks were made out and cashed for *phantom* employees.

35. Nonchalant [non-shun-**lahnt**]

adj def: appearing to be unconcerned; indifferent. (**)

Unlike the other players on the football team who pumped their fists when their names were announced, John ran on the field with a *nonchalant* wave.

36. Tinge [tinj]

verb syn: to color slightly.

Photographs become *tinged* with yellow as they age

37. Opulent [op-yuh-luhnt]

adj syn: rich; lavish. (**)

The mansion of newspaper tycoon Hearst is famous for its *opulent* décor.

38. Mutable [**myoo**-tuh-buhl]

adj syn: likely to change.

A politician's reputation can be highly *mutable*, as seen in the case of Harry Truman-mocked during his lifetime, revered afterward.

39. Forte [fawrt]

noun def: strong point, something a person does well. (***)

I do not know what her *forte* is, but it is not music.

40. Begrudge [bih-**gruhj**]
verb def: to envy or resent the pleasure or good fortune. (**)
She *begrudged* her friend's award.

41. Sympathy [**sim**-puh-thee]
noun def: favorable or approving account.
Alex viewed the pain with *sympathy* and publicly backed it.

42. Ethical [**eth**-i-kuhl]
adj def: pertaining to or dealing with morals.
It was not considered *ethical* for physicians to advertise.

43. Eloquence [**el**-uh-kwuhns]
noun def: fluent and effective speech. (*)
The Gettysburg Address is moving because of its lofty sentiments
as well as its *eloquence*.

44. Mediocrity [mee-dee-**ok**-ri-ties]
noun def: the state of being middling or poor in quality. (**)
The New York Mets, who had finished in ninth place in 1968,
won the world championship in 1969, going from horrible
to great in a single year and skipping *mediocrity*.

45. Clumsy [**kluhm**-zee]
adj def: awkward in movement.
Josh made a *clumsy* apology.

" *This book is revolutionary for studying for the SAT. I guess
this book will be the new bible for memorizing SAT words as
WordSmart was. Great book!!! GO AND BUY ONE!* **"**

Seongmin Oh *(Tenafly High School)*
Admitted to St. John's, Pharmacy

Synonym

1. Somber
        A) Joyous
        B) Depleted
        C) Multiply
        D) Undisputed
        E) Depress

2. Inadequate
        A) Competent
        B) Frugal
        C) Rescind
        D) Insufficient
        E) Offend

3. Exasperation
        A) Provocation
        B) Aggravation
        C) Arbitrary
        D) Verbal
        E) Laconic

4. Connive
        A) Scheme
        B) Cabal
        C) Virulent
        D) Salutary
        E) Precarious

5. Contempt

A) Antipathy
B) Mirth
C) Disdain
D) Adaptation
E) Sophistry

6. Cloak

A) Impudent
B) Probity
C) Largess
D) Coat
E) Precarious

7. Dubious

A) Doubt
B) Insult
C) Relating
D) Extol
E) Effusive

8. Concord

A) Pretext
B) Agree
C) Entangle
D) Alter
E) Grudge

Answer Keys

1) E   2) D   3) A   4) B   5) C   6) D   7) A   8) B

Antonym

1. Extravagant
    A) Indulgent
    B) Economical
    C) Provincial
    D) Indigenous
    E) Benign

2. Humble
    A) Meek
    B) Bashful
    C) Accurate
    D) Insolent
    E) Demure

3. Begrudge
    A) Strict
    B) Incompliant
    C) Generous
    D) Flexible
    E) Exploit

4. Nonchalant
    A) Intense
    B) Negligent
    C) Easygoing
    D) Magnified
    E) Enthrall

5. Begrudge
    A) Covet
    B) Stingy
    C) Timorous
    D) Monotony
    E) Likeness

6. Eloquence
A) Appeal
B) Dullness
C) Vivacity
D) Replicating
E) Forbid

7. Clumsy
A) Awkward
B) Gauche
C) Adroit
D) Indigenous
E) Accommodate

8. Bias
A) Consecration
B) Precursor
C) Integrate
D) Impartiality
E) Incarcerate

9. Opulent
A) Destitute
B) Infuriate
C) Euphoria
D) Insurrection
E) Peevish

Answer Keys

1) B   2) D   3) C   4) A   5) E   6) B   7) C   8) D   9) A

1. **Surreptitious** [sur-uhp-tish-uhs]
   adj def: characterized by secrecy. (*)
   > The Queen knew nothing of the *surreptitious* plots being hatched against her at court.

2. **Volatile** [**vol**-uh-tl]
   adj syn: quickly changing; fleeting; transitory; prone to violence. (***)
   > Public opinion is notoriously *volatile*; a politician who is very popular one month may be voted out of office the next.

3. **Conducive** [kuhn-**doo**-siv]
   adj syn: helpful; beneficial.
   > Practicing speaking English two hours a day is *conducive* for a language learner to develop proficiency.

4. **Override** [oh-ver-**rahyd**]
   verb def: to prevail or have dominance over. syn: nullify.
   > Mr. Johnson frequently *overrides* the boars' veto.

5. **Plight** [plahyt]
   noun def: a condition, state, or situation, especially an unfavorable one (**)
   > Having been unable to complete her task, she found herself in a sorry *plight*.

6. **Infatuated** [in-**fach**-oo-yet]
   verb def: strongly or foolishly attached to. (***)
   > After seeing the picture in a fashion magazine, Lester became completely *infatuated* with the beautiful model.

7. **Erratic** [ih-**rat**-ik]
   adj def: diverting from the usual or proper course in conduct.
   syn: eccentric; queer, erratic behavior.
   > John's *erratic* gesture made us think that he was weird.

8. **Forebode** [fawr-bohd]

   verb syn: to foretell or predict; an omen of. (***)

   Black clouds *forebode* a severe storm.

9. **Complacent** [kuhm-**pley**-suhnt]

   adj syn: self-satisfied; smug. (**)

   Phillip smiled *complacently* as he was showered with compliments
   for his handling of the Beckman deal.

10. **Sanctity** [**sangk**-ti-ties]

    noun syn: holiness; saintliness; godliness.

    The temple Sandy visited showed the inviolable *sanctity*.

11. **Demeanor** [dih-**mee**-ner]

    noun syn: conduct; behavior; deportment. (*)

    Not only does Lynn continuously show politeness to her friends,
    but she also always displays decent *demeanor* when she talks to
    other people.

12. **Fidgety** [**fij**-i-tee]

    adj syn: restless; impatient; uneasy. (**)

    Stephen has been considered as a *fidgety* person.

13. **Raunchy** [**rawn**-chee]

    adj syn: vulgar; crude; earthy; obscene.

    Steve embarrassed his friends by making a *raunchy* joke.

14. **Threshold** [**thresh**-ohld]

    noun def: any place or pointing of entering.

    Last year June started the *threshold* of a new teaching career.

15. **Voluptuous** [vuh-**luhp**-choo-uhs]

    adj def: full of pleasure and sensuous enjoyment. (**)

    Jessica's *voluptuous* life ruined her professional career.

16. Pandemonium [pan-duh-**moh**-nee-uhm]
noun syn: wild uproar or unrestrained disorder; tumult.
>By asking inappropriate questions in class, Jason frequently created a *pandemonium*.

17. Tribulation [trib-yuh-**ley**-shuhn]
noun syn: grievous trouble; severe trial or suffering. (***)
>John's inability to manage the situation put him in a serious *tribulation*.

18. Corollary [**kawr**-uh-ler-ee]
noun def: immediate consequence or easily drawn conclusion. (*)
>A *corollary* to the statement that a triangle is equilateral is that an equilateral triangle is also equiangular.

19. Precursor [pri-**kur**-ser]
noun syn: forefather; frontier; predecessor. (**)
>It is amazing to compare today's sleek, advanced computers with their bulky, slow *precursors*.

20. Sedition [si-**dish**-uhn]
noun def: incitement of discontent or rebellion against government.
>Brian was arrested for *sedition* after he gave a fiery speech condemning the government in the main square.

21. Insurrection [in-suh-**rek**-shuhn]
noun syn: rebellion.
>After the emperor's troops crushed the *insurrection*, its leader flew the country.

22. Subvert [suhb-**vurt**]
verb syn: to undermine; corrupt. (**)
>The traitor intended to *subvert* loyal citizens of the crown by distributing revolutionary propaganda.

23. **Consecrate** [**kon**-si-kreyt]
    verb def: the act of consecrating; to make or declare sacred.
    The minister *consecrated* the service on Sunday.

24. **Autonomy** [aw-**ton**-uh-mee]
    noun def: independence or freedom, the will or one's action.
    The rebels demanded *autonomy* from Spain.

25. **Efface** [ih-**feys**]
    verb syn: to erase; to make illegible. (***)
    Benjamin attempted to *efface* all traces of his troubled past
    by assuming a completely new identity.

26. **Tenacious** [tuh-**ney**-shuhs]
    adj syn: steadily pursuing a goal, unwilling to give up; stubborn.
    For years, against all odds, the company appeared to have a
    tenacious hold on the market.

27. **Manipulate** [muh-**nip**-yuh-leyt]
    verb syn: to manage or influence skillfully.
    He has a strong tendency to *manipulate* people's feelings.

28. **Determined** [dih-**tur**-mind]
    adj syn: resolute; staunch; decided; settled. (*)
    Daniel appears to be the *determined* defender of the Alamo.

29. **Descend** [dis-**send**]
    verb def: to go or pass from a higher to a lower place. (**)
    He slowly *descended* from the top of the mountain.

30. **Urchin** [**ur**-chin]
    noun syn: an elf; mischievous sprite.
    The *urchin* always sets numerous bad examples for his friends.

31. Inconspicuous [in-kuhn-**spik**-yoo-uhs]
adj syn: not noticeable, or prominent.
> By not talking in class, Jack was known as an
> *inconspicuous* student.

32. Tactful [**takt**-fuhl]
adj syn: skillful. (**)
> Lily tried to use a *tactful* technique to maintain
> the cordial relationships with her long-time clients.

33. Stifle [**stahy**-fuhl]
verb syn: to smother; suffocate; suppress.
> Although she longed to express her anger at the dictator,
> Maria *stifled* her protests in fear of being arrested.

34. Atrocity [uh-**tros**-i-tee]
noun def: horrible or usually brutal act.
> During the Indian bid for freedom from British colonial rule, a
> British officer committed the *atrocity* of slaughtering a large
> congregation of peaceful Indian demonstrators.

35. Discrepancy [dih-**skrep**-uhn-see]
noun def: a difference or variance between two or more things.
> The *discrepancies* between two witnesses' stories show that
> one of them must be lying.

36. Latitude [**lat**-i-tood]
noun def: freedom from narrow restrictions; freedom of action, opinion
> The judge appeared to have wide *latitude* to reject evidence
> for the trial.

37. Embrace [em-**breys**]
verb syn: to take in the arm; to include; to contain.
> An encyclopedia *embraces* a great number of subjects.

38. Gloat [goht]
verb def: to look at or think about with great or excessive. (***)
The opposing team *gloated* over our bad luck.

39. Exude [ig-**zood**]
verb syn: to give off; ooze.
The job candidate *exuded* an aura of self-confidence, impressing his interviewer.

40. Uncanny [uhn-**kan**-ee]
adj syn: mysterious; arousing superstitious fear or dread. (***)
Uncanny sounds filled the house.

41. Inexorable [in-**ek**-ser-uh-buhl]
adj syn: unable to be deterred; relentless. (**)
It is difficult to imagine how the mythic character of Oedipus could have avoided his evil destiny; his fate appears *inexorable*.

42. Engender [en-**jen**-der]
verb syn: to produce; to cause.
Countless disagreements over the proper use of national forests have *engendered* feelings of hostility between ranchers and environmentalists.

43. Stir [stur]
verb def: to move one's hand or implement continuously through.
Joe *stirred* his coffee until the sugar in the coffee completely dissolved.

44. Evoke [ih-**vohk**]
verb syn: to inspire memories; to produce a reaction. (*)
The sight of old elm tree *evoked* memories of the tree house she had built as a little girl.

45. **Connotation** [kon-uh-**tey**-shuhn]
    noun def: an act of instance of connoting, secondary meaning.
    A possible *connotation* of "home" is "A place of warmth, comfort, and affection."

46. **Patronage** [**pey**-truh-nij]
    noun def: condescending manner or attitude in granting favors. (***)
    The CEO of the company has an air of *patronage* toward his business subordinates.

"
Without a solid vocabulary foundation, students will struggle to attain a high score on the Critical Reading section of the SAT. William Shin's book is a collection of some of the most commonly used vocabulary words on the SAT and he facilitates students' memorization process by providing example sentences, concise multiple-choice questions, and a review of the more complex words. Memorize the words from cover to cover and you'll be prepared. "

Rosemari N. Lee
SAT Critical Reading Instructor

" Mastering Core SAT Words *is the epitome of what an SAT vocabulary book should be. For this comprehensive list of high-frequency words, Mr. Shin provides efficient definitions with which students can readily understand the nuance of each word. My favorite perk of this book is the ease of the pronunciation key. While knowing how to pronounce newly acquired vocabulary is crucial to effective and permanent retention, many books employ complex pronunciation keys alien to most students. By incorporating a key instinctively understood, Mr. Shin amplifies the efficacy of this book. I also strongly recommend that every student read through the addendum, "Analysis of the Reasoning SAT Questions," an insightful addition reflecting Mr. Shin's evident expertise. Students at any stages of their quests to SAT will benefit from* Mastering Core SAT Words. **"**

Han-Young Cho
SAT Critical Reading Instructor

" *From the countless number of books I've used and encountered to improve my vocabulary and critical reading skills, I can proudly say that Mr. Shin's newest book has been the most effective and helpful of all. I have never seen such a workbook be useful not only for SAT testing purposes, but also for intelligent daily conversations. As a student under the excellent and thorough instruction of Mr. Shin, I strongly advise students preparing for the SAT and also those who strive for a more developed vocabulary to use this book to its fullest.* **"**

Su Wan Kim
Paramus Catholic Regional High School

Synonym

1. Volatile
    A) Steadfast
    B) Provincial
    C) Extol
    D) Changeable
    E) Calm

2. Plight
    A) Complied
    B) Forbid
    C) Difficulty
    D) Arbitrary
    E) Repeal

3. Erratic
    A) Definite
    B) Aberrant
    C) Enact
    D) Tentative
    E) Discard

4. Complacent
    A) Calmness
    B) Dexterous
    C) Obsequious
    D) Exuberant
    E) Persuasive

5. Fidget
    A) Amorphous
    B) Equivocal
    C) Preeminent
    D) Viscous
    E) Restless

6. Voluptuous
    A) Bombastic
    B) Captivating
    C) Sensual Pleasure
    D) Lamentable
    E) Detect

7. Tribulation
    A) Adversity
    B) Unhappiness
    C) Curmudgeon
    D) Memento
    E) Suitor

8. Evoke
    A) Denude
    B) Arouse
    C) Matriculate
    D) Scrupulous
    E) Jocular

Answer keys

1) D 2) C 3) B 4) A 5) E 6) C 7) A 8) B

Antonym

1. Stir
- A) Abet
- B) Amend
- C) Approve
- D) Discourage
- E) Urge

2. Autonomy
- A) Independence
- B) Retreat
- C) Liability
- D) Intrusion
- E) Dependence

3. Determine
- A) Renewal
- B) Hesitate
- C) Rejection
- D) Ratification
- E) Exemplary

4. Tactful
- A) Careless
- B) Discreet
- C) Acclaimed
- D) Censure
- E) Orthodox

5. Discrepancy
- A) Conflict
- B) Hapless
- C) Concordance
- D) Berate
- E) Obscure

6. Engender
>   A) Arouse
>   B) Beget
>   C) Infamous
>   D) Halt
>   E) Relinquish

7. Patronage
>   A) Advocacy
>   B) Substitute
>   C) Laudatory
>   D) Rigid
>   E) Modesty

8. Override
>   A) Subvert
>   B) Approve
>   C) Contemplate
>   D) Mar
>   E) Elusive

9. Uncanny
>   A) Common
>   B) Betray
>   C) Peevish
>   D) Tawdry
>   E) Baleful

Answer keys

1) D   2) E   3) B   4) A   5) C   6) D   7) E   8) B   9) A

1. **Barter** [**bahr**-ter]
   verb def: to exchange in trade, as one commodity for another.
   Tom is *bartering* away his pride for material gain.

2. **Incoherent** [in-koh-**heer**-uhnt]
   adj syn: the quality or state of being inconsistent.
   The *incoherent* remark Tom made confused everyone in the office.

3. **Intuition** [in-too-**ish**-uhn]
   noun def: direct perception of truth.
   Tim seems to have a sharp *intuition* about people.

4. **Sophistry** [**sof**-uh-stree]
   noun syn: a false argument. (**)
   Alice uses a *sophistry* tactic when she convinces her parents.

5. **Supplementary** [suhp-luh-**men**-tah-ree]
   adj syn: additional.
   Vitamins were introduced as *supplementary* pills to people.

6. **Integrate** [**in**-ti-greyt]
   verb syn: to combine; to incorporate.
   The principal attempted to *integrate* minority groups into
   the school system.

7. **Substantiate** [suhb-**stan**-shee-yet]
   verb def: to affirm as having substance; give body to strength. (***)
   Telling a lie *substantiates* a false friendship.

8. **Tonal** [tohn-l]
   adj def: relating to pitch or sound. (*)
   Although it has interesting lyrics, the song's *tonal* problem makes
   it unpleasant to listen to.

9. Remedy [rem-i-dee]
verb syn: to cure; correct. (**)
> We can *remedy* this disaster by putting our emergency backup plan into effect right away.

10. Reinforce [ree-in-force]
verb def: to strengthen with some added pieces. syn: to augment.
> The Prime Minister decided to dispatch additional troops to *reinforce* the ability to suppress rebellions.

11. Epitome [ih-pit-uh-mee]
noun def: representative of an entire group. syn: synopsis; summary. (***)
> The host was the *epitome* of graciousness, making his entire guests feel perfectly comfortable.

12. Proponent [pruh-poh-nuhnt]
noun syn: advocate; defender; supporter. (**)
> A devoted *proponent* of animal rights, Rose rescued stray dogs and cats at every opportunity.

13. Embodiment [em-bod-ee-muhnt]
noun def: the state of expression
verb def: to give a concrete form to express; to make corporeal.
> Lim *embodies* an idea in an allegorical painting.

14. Debunk [dih-buhngk]
verb syn: to discredit; disprove. (**)
> It was the teacher's mission in life to *debunk* the myth that girls are bad at math.

15. Trifling [trahy-fling]
adj syn: insignificant; trivial. (***)
> That little glitch in the computer program is a *trifling* error; in general, it works really well.

16. Irreverent [ih-**rev**-er-uhnt]
adj syn: disrespectful. (**)

> Kevin's *irreverent* attitude in Sunday school annoyed the priest, but amused the other children.

17. Arcane [ahr-**keyn**]
adj syn: mysterious; obscure.

> Eliot's "Waste Land" is filled with *arcane* lore, including quotations in Latin, Greek, French, German, and Sanskrit.

18. Abstruse [ab-**stroos**]
adj syn: difficult to comprehend. (**)

> The philosopher's elucidation was so clear that he turned an *abstruse* subject into one his audience could grasp.

19. Didactic [dahy-**dak**-tik]
adj syn: intended to teach; instructive. (***)

> The children's TV show Sesame Street is designed to be both entertaining and *didactic*.

20. Lucid [**loo**-sid]
adj syn: clear and easily understood.

> Explanations should be written in a *lucid* manner so that people can understand them.

21. Xenophobia [zen-uh-**foh**-bee-uh]
noun def: fear or hatred of foreigners or strangers.

> Countries in which *xenophobia* is prevalent often have more restrictive immigration policies than countries that are more open to foreign influences.

22. Insolence [**in**-suh-luhns]
noun def: an attitude or behavior that is bold and disrespectful. (***)

> Some feel that reporters who shout questions at the president are behaving with *insolence*.

23. Virtue [vur-choo]
noun syn: moral excellence; goodness; righteousness.
Stephen has never lost his *virtue* even after college.

24. Repeal [ri-peel]
verb syn: to revoke; formally withdraw (often a law). (***)
The U.S. government *repealed* the Prohibition when it was
obvious that the law was not functioning as it had been intended.

25. Solemn [sol-uhm]
adj syn: grave; sober; mirthless as a person. (*)
Listening to *solemn* music makes people feel very sad.

26. Ruthless [rooth-lis]
adj def: without pity or compassion.
Hitler is known as a *ruthless* dictator.

27. Relentless [ri-lent-lis]
adj syn: severe; strict; unrelenting. (**)
Ancient people learned to survive in a *relentless* environment.

28. Subservient [suh b-sur-vee-uh-nt]
adj def: servile; excessively submissive, obsequious; subservient persons
Henson and Stowe did become close friends, and Stowe herself
drew direct parallels between Uncle Tom and Josiah Henson.
Sadder still, the term "Uncle Tom" has since taken on negative,
minstrel-show connotations of *subservient* blacks kowtowing to
whites, which is unfortunate, because it undermines the triumph
that was Josiah Henson's life. He was no caricature, and his
achievements were real.
    —Will Ferguson, Beauty Tips From Moose Jaw, 2004

29. Exquisite [ik-skwiz-it]
adj syn: extraordinary; keenly; delicately sensitive.
Timothy has an *exquisite* ear for music.

30. Oblivious [uh-**bliv**-ee-uhs]
adj syn: unaware; inattentive. (**)
>   Gandhi calmly made his way through the crowd, seemingly
>   *oblivious* to the angry rioters around him.

31. Contemplate [kon-**tuhm**-pleyt]
verb syn: to consider thoroughly; think fully.
>   Timothy spent hours *contemplating* on a difficult problem.

32. Whimsical [**hwim**-zi-kuhl]
adj syn: playful or fanciful idea. (***)
>   The ballet was *whimsical*, delighting the children with
>   its imaginative characters and unpredictable sets.

33. Theorem [**thee**-er-uhm]
noun syn: an idea; belief; method.
>   A *theorem* is generally accepted as true or worthwhile
>   without proof.

34. Reproach [ri-**prohch**]
verb syn: to find fault with; blame. (*)
>   Renee *reproached* her boyfriend for forgetting to buy her
>   a Christmas present.

35. Cynic [**sin**-ik]
noun def: person who distrusts the movies of others.
>   Have we become a nation of *cynics* who have lost faith in our
>   own system of government?

36. Nefarious [ni-**fair**-ee-uhs]
adj syn: vicious; evil. (**)
>   *Nefarious* deeds are never far from an evildoer's mind.

37. Byzantine [**biz**-uhn-teen]
adj def: a characterized by elaborating scheming and intrigue.
>   Staring at the *Byzantine* church, John began to talk to the bishop
>   standing next him.

38. Multifarious [muhl-tuh-**fair**-ee-ubs]

adj syn: diverse.

Ken opened the hotel room window, letting in the *multifarious* noises of the great city.

39. Lackadaisical [lak-uh-**dey**-zi-kuhl]

adj syn: idle, lazy; apathetic; indifferent. (*)

The clerk yawned openly in the customer's face, not bothering to hide his *lackadaisical* attitude.

40. Yoke [yohk]

verb syn: to join together; harness a draft. (***)

As soon as the farmer had *yoked* his oxen together, he began to plow the field.

41. Slipshod [**slip**-shod]

adj syn: careless; hasty.

Because she was so stressed out, Kirk did a rather *slipshod* job on his last project.

42. Compulsive [kuhm-**puhl**-siv]

adj syn: obsessive; fanatic. (**)

A *compulsive* liar, Reggie told his boss that he had once climbed Mount Everest with a yak on his back.

43. Deviate [**dee**-vee-yet]

verb syn: to stray; wonder.

As long as you do not *deviate* from the trail, you should be fine out in the wilderness.

44. Retrieve [ri-**treev**]

verb syn: to bring; fetch; reclaim.

The eager Labrador *retrieved* the Frisbee from the lake.

45. Anachronistic [uh-nak-ruh-**nis**-tik]

adj syn: out of the proper time.

The reference in Shakespeare's Julius Caesar to "the clock striking twelve" is *anachronistic* because there were no striking timepieces in ancient Rome.

Synonym

1. Incoherence
    A) Fawn
    B) Incongruity
    C) Servile
    D) Abstemious
    E) Sterilize

2. Integrate
    A) Divide
    B) Mendacious
    C) Amalgamate
    D) Cloister
    E) Maverick

3. Proponent
    A) Altruist
    B) Banality
    C) Demagogue
    D) Advocate
    E) Vanity

4. Debunk
    A) Demystify
    B) Sycophant
    C) Omnivore
    D) Deplete
    E) Hoard

5. Trifling
A) Dull
B) Vile
C) Wholesome
D) Inconceivable
E) Insignificant

6. Irreverent
A) Debilitate
B) Disrespect
C) Augur
D) Exonerate
E) Stern

7. Abstruse
A) Sympathy
B) Eloquent
C) Difficult to understand
D) Terseness
E) Confidence

8. Compulsive
A) Compelling
B) Aptitude
C) Eccentric
D) Valor
E) Agonize

Answer Keys

1) B   2) C   3) D   4) A   5) E   6) B   7) C   8) A

Antonym

1. Insolence
    A) Wary
    B) Inured
    C) Modesty
    D) Receptive
    E) Agile

2. Solemn
    A) Passive
    B) Capricious
    C) Attentive
    D) Frivolous
    E) Arduous

3. Relentless
    A) Adamant
    B) Adage
    C) Displacing
    D) Convoluted
    E) Intermittent

4. Reproach
    A) Approval
    B) Antagonistic
    C) Prompting
    D) Influential
    E) Thwart

5. Nefarious
    A) Abominable
    B) Illegible
    C) Respectable
    D) Haphazard
    E) Oral

6. Lackadaisical
>A) Acute
>B) Restricted
>C) Diffuse
>D) Energetic
>E) Fatal

7. Slipshod
>A) Feeble
>B) Neat
>C) Perfunctory
>D) Docile
>E) Calculating

8. Yoke
>A) Invoke
>B) Debilitate
>C) Quack
>D) Desultory
>E) Disconnect

9. Oblivious
>A) Aware
>B) Adept
>C) Mock
>D) Diverse
>E) Unison

Answer Keys

1) C 2) D 3) E 4) A 5) C 6) D 7) B 8) E 9) A

1. ## Testament [tes-**tuh**-muhnt]
   noun syn: statement of belief; will.
   > Gary's children could not believe that he left everything to his Chihuahua in his last will and *testament*.

2. ## Vapid [**vap**-id]
   adj syn: tedious; dull. (***)
   > Kenneth found his blind date to be *vapid* and boring, and couldn't wait to get away from her.

3. ## Totalitarian [toh-tal-i-**tair**-ee-uhn]
   adj def: exercising control over the freedom, will.
   > The *totalitarian* government does not tolerate parties with differing opinions.

4. ## Regime [ruh-**zheem**]
   noun def: a ruling or prevailing system.
   > North Korea has been dictated by a dictatorial *regime* for the past fifty years.

5. ## Indict [in-**dahyt**]
   verb def: to bring a formal accusation against. syn: accuse.
   > The grand jury *indicted* him for murder.

6. ## Mock [mok]
   verb syn: to challenge; defy; attack. (**)
   > His action *mocks* convention.

7. ## Adept [uh-**dept**]
   adj syn: very skilled; proficient.
   > Eric appears to be an *adept* juggler.

8. ## Seraphic [si-**raf**-ik]
   adj syn: angelic; pure; sublime. (**)
   > Selena's sweet, *seraphic* appearance belied her nasty, bitter personality.

9. Reclusive [rek-loos-siv]
adj def: shut off from the world. syn: hermit. (**)

Anthony's *reclusive* tendencies led him to leave the city and move into a lonely cabin in Montana.

10. Amass [uj-mas]
verb def: to gather for oneself; collect as one's own. syn: accumulate.

He *amassed* his papers for his memoirs.

11. Cutlery [kuht-luh-ree]
noun def: cutting instrument.

The restaurant was notorious for not washing its *cutlery* properly.

12. Assess [uh-ses]
verb syn: to evaluate; estimate; determine.

Dr. Goldenberg *assesses* his students' academic capabilities by having them take a practice test on Fridays.

13. Penchant [pen-chuhnt]
noun syn: inclination; tendency. (**)

Tiffany had a *penchant* for sitting by the window and staring off into space.

14. Savory [sey-vuh-ree]
adj def: aggreable in taste or smell. (***)

The banquet guests consumed the *savory* treats with pleasure.

15. Predilection [pred-l-ek-shuhn]
noun syn: preference; liking. (**)

The old woman's *predilection* for candy was evident from the chocolate bar wrappers strewn all over her apartment.

16. Raid [reyd]
verb syn: a sudden attack; assault.

The general *raided* the enemy's military base.

17. Prestige [pre-**steezh**]
noun syn: reputation. def: influencing arising from success.
>The new discotheque has great *prestige* with the jet set.

18. Profound [**pruh**-found]
adj def: penetrating or entering deeply into subjects of thought. (**)
>Unlike other people, Joe has a tremendously *profound* insight.

19. Detach [dih-**tach**]
verb syn: to separate; unfasten; disengage; disunite.
>The commanding officer decided to *detach* a couple of battleships on a special mission.

20. Perquisite [**pur**-kwuh-zit]
noun syn: benefit; privilege; gratuity. (**)
>Homage was once the *perquisite* of loyalty.

21. Monastic [muh-**nas**-tik]
adj def: extremely plain or secluded, as in a monastery.
>The philosopher retired to his *monastic* lodgings to contemplate life free from any worldly distraction.

22. Tribulation [trib-yuh-**ley**-shuhn]
noun syn: grievous trouble; severe trial or suffering. (***)
>Jeffrey has gone through a number of *tribulations* since last September.

23. Irreproachable [ir-i-**proh**-chuh-buhl]
adj syn: free from blame. (****)
>John's recent statement about freedom of speech in public turned out to be *irreproachable*.

24. Hodgepodge [**hoj**-poj]
noun def: a heterogeneous mixture; jumble
>Jack was really shocked because the exhibit he visited was a *hodgepodge* of mediocre art, bad art, and really bad art.

25. Affliction [uh-**frik**-shuhn]
noun def: a state of pain
verb syn: to distress with mental or bodily pain. (*)
    The old man has been *afflicted* with arthritis.

26. Commend [kuh-**mend**]
verb syn: to present; mention; or praise as worthy of confidence.
    The captain *commended* a soldier for bravery.

27. Ultimate [**uhl**-tuh-mit]
adj syn: last; furthest or farthest; ending a process or series.
    Tom has just completed the *ultimate* point in his journey.

28. Classify [**klas**-uh-fahy]
verb def: to arrange or organize by classes; order according to class.
    Dr. Phil spent numerous hours to *classify* a variety of trees
    and plants.

29. Inquiry [in-**kwahy**-ree]
noun syn: query; investigation. def: a seeking or request for truth.
    The *inquiry* conducted by a local newspaper led police personnel
    to be able to find the serial killer.

30. Heterodox [**het**-er-uh-doks]
adj syn: unorthodox; unconventional. (**)
    To those who upheld the belief that Earth did not move, Galileo's
    theory that Earth circles the Sun was disturbingly *heterodox*.

31. Enmity [**en**-mi-tee]
noun syn: ill will; hatred.
    At Camp David, President Carter labored to bring an end to
    the *enmity* that prevented Egypt and Israel from living in peace.

32. Cynical [**sin**-i-kuhl]
adj syn: sarcastic; sneer.
    John appears to have a *cynical* disposition toward the poor.

33. Resent [ri-zent]
verb syn: indignation; insult. (**)
> Mr. Chung was *resented* by a huge lie made by Stephen last week.

34. Cite [sahyt]
verb syn: to quote as an authority; to mention.
> He *cited* the Constitution in his defense.

35. Indignant [in-dig-nuhnt]
adj def: expressing strong displeasure at something considered unjust. (***)
> After paying a large sum of money to John, Peter showed an *indignant* expression on his face.

36. Outlandish [out-lan-dish]
adj syn: foreign; bizarre; alien; odd.
> Jonathan was extremely excited by the *outlandish* scene he had never seen before.

37. Enchant [en-chant]
verb def: to delight to a high degree.
> Her gaiety and wit have *enchanted* us all.

38. Crank [krangk]
noun syn: eccentric, whimsical notion. (**)
> Alex did not mean to make a *crank* in a response to the announcement the principal made this morning.

39. Alteration [awl-tuh-rey-shuhn]
noun def: the act or process of altering; the state of being altered.
> The *alteration* will improve the dress.

40. Politic [pol-i-tik]
adj def: discreet; tactful.
> Her prudent and *politic* management of the crisis led her to be elected president the following year.

41. Pore [pawr]

verb syn: to exam; to scrutinize. (**)
Jason *pored* over the strange events of the preceding evening.

42. Implausible [im-**plaw**-zuh-buhl]

adj syn: improbable; inconceivable. (***)
A skeptical man by nature, Max found his neighbor's claim that
he had seen a UFO highly *implausible*.

43. Envisage [en-**viz**-ij]

verb syn: to contemplate; visualize.
Professor Phillip *envisaged* an era of great scientific discoveries.

44. Diverse [dih-**vurs**]

adj def: a different kind, form, or character.
People seem to have a wide range of *diverse* opinions
about education.

45. Unison [**yoo**-nuh-suhn]

noun def: coincidence in pitch of two or more musical tones.
Male and female voices in the opera are amazingly in *unison*.

" *Containing a massive number of 1,395 core SAT words,*
this book provides students with a priceless list. Synonyms,
definitions, and example sentences help students to have a
greater understanding of the words. With Mr. William Shin's
experience as an SAT instructor and his unconditional love
for his students, this book is indeed at the base of the pathway
leading to success in the SAT. **"**

Sarah Lee (Bergen County Academies)
Admitted to New York University, Hotel Management

Synonym

1. Vapid
   A) Gregarious
   B) Antagonistic
   C) Dull
   D) Frugal
   E) Dependable

2. Mock
   A) Counterfeit
   B) Argument
   C) Conjecture
   D) Tenuous
   E) Saturnine

3. Adept
   A) Melancholy
   B) Adroit
   C) Querulous
   D) Bonhomie
   E) Eloquent

4. Reclusive
   A) Vitriol
   B) Affable
   C) Convivial
   D) Unsociable
   E) Choler

5. Savory

    A) Animated
    B) Didactic
    C) Expatriate
    D) Radical
    E) Delectable

6. Profound

    A) Sophisticated
    B) Deep
    C) Magnificent
    D) Denigrate
    E) Tentative

7. Perquisite

    A) Concede
    B) Superb
    C) Largess
    D) Indifferent
    E) Compelling

8. Envisage

    A) Languid
    B) Humane
    C) Meager
    D) Captivate
    E) Contemplate

Answer Keys

1) C 2) A 3) B 4) D 5) E 6) B 7) C 8) E

Antonym

1. Tribulation
  A) Suffering
  B) Happiness
  C) Dictate
  D) Transmit
  E) Illustrious

2. Affliction
  A) Dissemination
  B) Relevant
  C) Accurate
  D) Consolation
  E) Inventive

3. Heterodox
  A) Laconic
  B) Pithy
  C) Orthodox
  D) Obtuse
  E) Pragmatic

4. Resent
  A) Happy
  B) Esoteric
  C) Trite
  D) Monotonous
  E) Naïve

5. Indignant
  A) Effective
  B) Gleeful
  C) Redundant
  D) Awkward
  E) Opulent

6. Alteration
- A) Ascorbic
- B) Varying
- C) Provincial
- D) No change
- E) Ignored

7. Implausible
- A) Peripheral
- B) Inconsequential
- C) Believable
- D) Depraved
- E) Acrimonious

8. Pore
- A) Insurgent
- B Sagacious
- C) Mundane
- D) Scoff
- E) Scan

9. Enmity
- A) Affinity
- B) Mirth
- C) Deem
- D) Subterfuge
- E) Cynic

Answer keys

1) B   2) D   3) C   4) A   5) B   6) D   7) C   8) E   9) A

1. **Influx** [in-fluhks]
noun def: an act of flowing in.

An *influx* of tourists to this town will dramatically increase because of the discoveries made by anthropologists.

2. **Delineation** [dih-lin-ee-ey-shuhn]
noun syn: depiction; representation. (**)

Mrs. Baxter was very satisfied with the artist's *delineation* of her.

3. **Penumbra** [pi-nuhm-bruh]
noun def: partial shadow.

The *penumbras* of the spooky forest frightened Dorothy and her dog, Toto.

4. **Quack** [kwak]
noun syn: faker; one who falsely claims to have medical skill. (***)

Licenses are given to doctors so that patients can be assured that their M.D.'s are qualified professionals rather than *quacks*.

5. **Disclaim** [dis-kleym]
verb syn: to deny; repudiate; disavow. (*)

Peterson *disclaimed* the fact that he had an inappropriate relationship with his secretary.

6. **Grasp** [grasp]
verb syn: to perceive and understand; to hold securely. (***)

Peggy could not *grasp* the concept that Dwight had dumped her, and she continued to call him everyday.

7. **Invoke** [in-vohk]
verb syn: to call upon; request; help.

Lily *invoked* the financial assistance of all her relatives when her business ran into serious trouble.

8. **Rebuff** [ri-buhf]
verb syn: blunt rejection; to refute; to deny. (****)

The princess coldly *rebuffed* her suitor's marriage proposal, turning her back on him and walking away.

9. **Estrange** [ih-**streynj**]

verb syn: to alienate; to keep at a distance. (**)

Estranged from his family for years, Allan had not heard that both his parents had passed away.

10. **Geometric** [jee-uh-**me**-trik]

adj def: resembling or employing the simple rectilinear or curvilinear lines or figures used in geometry.

Tom made a solid determination to decorate his room with a *geometric* pattern no matter what his mother said.

11. **Reveal** [ri-**veel**]

verb syn: to expose; to make known; to disclose; to divulge.

Albert had no intention to *reveal* his secret to his friends.

12. **Gullible** [**guhl**-uh-buhl]

adj syn: easily deceived; cheated. (**)

The *gullible* landlord believed Rich's story that he was only going away for a few days, despite the moving boxes that littered the apartment.

13. **Endue** [en-**dyoo**]

verb def: to invest or endow with some gift, quality, or beauty

Hamlet *endued* the character of a madman.

14. **Provocative** [pruh-**vok**-uh-tiv]

adj def: likely to stimulate emotion, ideas or controversy.

The demonstrators began to chant obscenities, a *provocative* act that they hoped would cause the police to lose control.

15. **Hierarchy** [**hahy**-uh-rahr-kee]

noun syn: a ranking of people, an idea from highest to lowest.

A cabinet secretary ranks just below the president and vice president in the *hierarchy* of the executive branch.

16. Evolve [ih-**loo**-siv]

verb syn: to develop gradually.

> The human species *evolved* from an ancestor that was properly arboreal.

17. Conceive [kuhn-**seev**]

verb syn: to form a notion or ideas; to imagine. (*)

> He *conceived* the project while he was on vacation.

18. Patronize [**pey**-truh-nahyz]

verb syn: to condescend; disparage; belittle. (***)

> LuAnn *patronized* the students, treating them like idiots, which they deeply resented.

19. Discretionary [dih-**skresh**-uh-ner-ee]

adj def: subject to own judgment.

> Ambassadors have some *discretionary* powers; however, they must bow to the authority of the secretary of state

20. Agnostic [ag-**nos**-tik]

noun def: one who doubts that God exists.

> When she could find no evidence to affirm the existence of God, she proclaimed herself an *agnostic*.

21. Eclectic [ih-**klek**-tik]

adj syn: drawn from many sources; varied; heterogeneous. (**)

> The Mellon family art collection is an *eclectic* one, including works ranging from ancient Greek sculptures to modern paintings.

22. Quixotic [kwik-**sot**-ik]

adj syn: overly idealistic; impractical. (***)

> The practical Danuta was skeptical of her roommate's *quixotic* plans to build a rollercoaster in their yard.

23. Foster [**faw**-ster]

verb syn: to promote; encourage; develop.

> Grace *fostered* her only child in an educational environment.

24. Allege [uh-**lej**]
verb syn: to assert without proof.
> An increasing number of scientists *allege* that the Earth will collide into a comet by 2100.

25. Ascertain [as-er-**teyn**]
verb syn: to determine; discover; make certain of. (**)
> Although he tried with all his might, the archaeologist could not *ascertain* the correct age of the Piltown man's skeleton.

26. Infectious [in-**fek**-shuhs]
adj def: communicable by infection.
> During the 1960's, a number of people were suffering from an unknown *infectious* disease.

27. Presumption [pri-**zuhmp**-shuhn]
noun def: the act of presuming, belief on reasonable ground.
> Albert made a *presumption* that more immigrants will face tremendous difficultly obtaining green cards from the government of the United States.

28. Demagogue [**dem**-uh-gog]
noun def: a leader who plays dishonestly on the prejudices and emotion of followers.
> Senator Joseph McCarthy was labeled a *demagogue* who used the paranoia of the anti- Communist 1950s as a way of seizing fame and power in Washington.

29. Subdued [suhb-**dood**]
adj syn: suppressed; stifled. (***)
> The actor was momentarily *subdued* after the director yelled at him, but soon enough, he was his usual confident self again.

30. Indigenous [in-**dij**-uh-nuhs]
adj syn: native, occurring naturally in an area. (**)
> Palm trees, unlike penguins, are *indigenous* to Florida.

31. Transitory [tran-si-tawr-ee]
adj syn: quickly passing.

Public moods tend to be *transitory*; people may be anxious and angry one month, but relatively content and optimistic the next.

32. Pliant [plahy-uhnt]
adj syn: pliable; yielding. (**)

Only those with extremely *pliant* limbs are able to perform complex yoga moves.

33. Arboreal [ahr-bawr-ee-uhl]
adj syn: related to trees; living in trees. (*)

The squirrel is an *arboreal* mammal, spending much of its time running up and down trees.

34. Steadfast [sted-fast]
adj syn: unwavering; resolution; faith.

Tom and Susan appear to have a *steadfast* relationship with each other.

35. Unwitting [uhn-wit-ing]
adj syn: unconscious; unintentional. (**)

Not looking where he was going, John *unwittingly* charged into the subway car.

36. Elusive [ih-loo-siv]
adj syn: hard to capture, grasp, or understanding. (***)

Though everyone thinks they know what "justice" is, when one tries to define the concept precisely, it proves to be quite *elusive*.

37. Antagonistism [an-tag-uh-niz-uhm]
noun syn: hostility; conflict; opposition.

As more and more reporters investigated the Watergate Scandal, *antagonism* between Nixon and the Press increased.

38. Condense [kuhn-dens]
verb def: to reduce to a shorter term.

Sullivan always *condensed* his answer into a few words.

39. Extol [ik-**stohl**]
verb syn: a greatly praise. (**)
At the party convention, speaker after speaker rose to *extol* their candidate for the presidency.

40. Pseudonym [**sood**-n-im]
noun syn: pen name; fictitious.
The expose was so thoroughly damning to all parties involved that the author was forced to publish it under a *pseudonym*.

41. Furtive [fur-**tiv**]
adj syn: secret; stealthy. (***)
Jennifer and Phillip exchanged *furtive* smiles across the table.

42. Venal [**veen**-l]
adj def: willing to sell one's influence. (**)
The corrupted police office made a *venal* agreement with a gang member.

43. Startle [**stahr**-tle]
verb def: to disturb by surprise or alarm.
The noise from the kitchen *startled* John, who was sleeping in his room.

44. Mischievous [mis-**chuh**-vuhs]
adj syn: vexation; annoying.
The teacher was really upset about one of his students' *mischievous* behavior in class.

45. Decipher [dis-**sahy**-fer]
verb def: to discover of the meaning of anything obscure.
The archeologist tried to *decipher* hieroglyphics.

Synonym

1.Quack
    A) Genuine
    B) Redundant
    C) Counterfeit
    D) Opulent
    E) Acerbic

2. Grasp
    A) Prudent
    B) Understand
    C) Reticent
    D) Pastoral
    E) Derivative

3. Rebuff
    A) Endemic
    B) Credulous
    C) Infirmary
    D) Denial
    E) Servile

4. Reveal
    A) Exposed
    B) Agnostic
    C) Abstemious
    D) Mendacious
    E) Syndicate

5. Gullible

     A) Omnivore

     B) Carnivore

     C) Naïve

     D) Dull

     E) Augur

6. Patronize

     A) Exonerate

     B) Condescend

     C) Verdict

     D) Exaggerate

     E) Compassionate

7. Eclectic

     A) Eloquent

     B) Enraged

     C) Attitude

     D) Barren

     E) Assorted

8. Estrange

     A) Alienate

     B) Adumbrate

     C) Disintegrate

     D) Perplex

     E) Culpable

Answer Keys

1) C 2) B 3) D 4) A 5) C 6) B 7) E 8) A

Antonym

1. Allege
> A) Dissent
> B) Redressing
> C) Flouting
> D) Zenith
> E) Sham

2. Subdued
> A) Pinnacle
> B) Decline
> C) Boisterous
> D) Fiasco
> E) Dearth

3. Transitory
> A) Controversial
> B) Spate
> C) Influx
> D) Permanent
> E) Generic

4. Steadfast
> A) Trenchant
> B) Unreliable
> C) Elongated
> D) Abstruse
> E) Abandoned

5. Condense
> A) Enlarge
> B) Indicted
> C) Exculpated
> D) Exhumed
> E) Rescinded

6. Furtive
A) Tacit
B) Forthright
C) Speculative
D) Unwitting
E) Ambiguous

7. Startle
A) Audacity
B) Prestige
C) Concise
D) Calm
E) Fidelity

8. Ascertain
A) Check
B) Deplore
C) Overlook
D) Loquacious
E) Taciturn

9. Foster
A) Concord
B) Amalgamate
C) Ominous
D) Insolence
E) Condemn

Answer Keys

1) A 2) C 3) D 4) B 5) A 6) B 7) D 8) C 9) E

1. **Glean** [gleen]
   verb syn: to gather; discover; collect. (*)
   > Farmers spend many hours *gleaning* the crop that they cultivated.

2. **Speculative** [Spek-yuh-ley-tiv]
   adj syn: involving assumption; uncertain; theoretical. (***)
   > The theories Paul is presenting are purely *speculative,* and people should not be acted upon until more research has been done to test them out.

3. **Epidemic** [ep-i-dem-ik]
   adj def: extremely prevalence or rapid spread.
   > A variety of *epidemic* diseases suddenly occurred in 1945.

4. **Rigorous** [rig-er-uhs]
   adj syn: severity; harsh.
   > Tim knows how to survive in a *rigorous* environment.

5. **Render** [ren-der]
   verb syn: to describe; to represent. (**)
   > Yuri attempted to *render* a painting as vividly as possible.

6. **Aspersion** [uh-spur-zhuhn]
   noun def: false rumor, damaging report.
   > It is unfair to cast *aspersion* on someone behind his or her back.

7. **Accouter** [uh-koo-ter]
   verb def: to equip or outfit, especially with military clothes
   > Most of the hikers I encountered *accoutered* with walking sticks, water bottles, trail maps, and compasses.

8. **Grudge** [gruhj]
   noun def: a feeling of will or resentment.
   > Ashley holds a strong *grudge* against a former opponent.

9. **Staunch** [stawnch]
   adj syn: resolute; dependable; ardent; faithful. (**)
   > He delivered a *staunch* defense of the government.

10. Dire [dahyuh]
adj def: causing or involving great fear or suffering; dreadful; terrible.
Mr. Greenspan made a *dire* prediction about the stock market.

11. Neglect [ni-**glekt**]
verb def: to pay no attention or too little attention to; disregard.
The public *neglected* his genius mind for many years.

12. Coerced [koh-**urs**]
verb syn: to compel by force; intimidation. (*)
The thief *coerced* the cashier into handing over all the money in the cash register.

13. Disincline [dis-in-**klahyn**]
verb syn: to make or be averse or unwilling.
Your rudeness *disinclines* me to grant your request.

14. Circumvent [sur-kuhm-**vent**]
verb syn: to go around; avoid. (**)
Laura *circumvented* the hospital's visiting schedule, slipping into her boyfriend's room long after visiting hours were over.

15. Supple [**suhp**-uhl]
adj syn: flexible; pliant.
The *supple* stalks of bamboo swayed back and forth in the wind.

16. Ameliorate [uh-**meel**-yuh-reyt]
verb syn: to make better; to improve.
Hiring dozens of expertly trained nurses *ameliorated* conditions in the hospital.

17. Belabor [bih-**ley**-ber]
verb syn: to insist repeatedly or harp on. (**)
I understand completely; you do not need to *belabor* the point.

18. **Condone** [kuhn-**dohn**]

> *verb* syn: to pardon, forgive; overlook, justify, or excuse a fault. (**)
> "We can not *condone* your behavior," said Raj's parents after
> he missed his curfew. "You are grounded."

19. **Tame** [teym]

> *adj* def: change from the wild or savage state. syn: domesticated. (***)
> That lion acts as *tame* as a house cat.

20. **Gluttony** [**gluht**-n-ee]

> *noun* def: eating and drinking to excess. syn: voracious. (**)
> It took days for the guests to recover their appetites after the
> *gluttony* that had taken place at the party.

21. **Adroit** [uh-**droit**]

> *adj* syn: skillful; accomplished.
> The *adroit* athlete completed even the most difficult obstacle
> course with ease.

22. **Nihilism** [**nahy**-uh-liz-uhm]

> *noun* def: belief that existence and all traditional values are meaningless.
> Robert's *nihilism* expressed itself in his lack of concern with
> the norms of a decent, moral society.

23. **Foreshadow** [fawr-**shad**-oh]

> *verb* def: to shadow or indicate beforehand.
> Political upheavals *foreshadowed* war.

24. **Paucity** [**paw**-si-tee]

> *noun* syn: scarcity; lack; penury. (**)
> Because of the relative *paucity* of bananas in the country, their
> price was very high.

25. **Barrage** [buh-**rahzh**]

> *noun* def: overwhelming quantity or explosion.
> He prepared a *barrage* of questions to justify what Stephen
> had done in the meeting.

26. Libertine [lib-er-teen]
noun def: one who believes in unrestricted freedom. (*)

The *libertine* took pleasure in gambling and seducing innocent youth.

27. Orderly [awr-der-lee]
adj def: arranged or disposed in a neat, tidy manner.

Tim always maintains his desk in an *orderly* fashion.

28. Preclude [prel-yood]
verb syn: to rule out.

The seriousness of the damage to the car *precluded* any attempt to repair it; it had to be scrapped.

29. Abase [uh-beys]
verb syn: humble; disgrace. (**)

After his immature behavior, John was *abased* in my eyes.

30. Consolidate [kuhn-sol-i-deyt]
verb syn: to combine; incorporate.

The author *consolidated* various articles she had previously published into one book.

31. Compound [kom-pound]
adj def: composed of two or more parts, elements, or ingredient.

Soap is a *compound* substance.

32. Rebut [ri-buht]
verb syn: to refute; to deny; to decline. (***)

The moderator was careful to allow sufficient time for callers to *rebut* claims made by her guest speakers.

33. Startle [stahr-tl]
verb def: to disturb or agitate suddenly as by surprise. (**)

Josh began to be *startled* by the fact that he might not be able to meet Lynn anymore.

34. Motley [mot-lee]
adj def: many colored; composed of diverse parts. (**)
> The club was made up of a *motley* crew of people from all kinds of different backgrounds.

35. Recurrence [ri-kur-uh ns]
noun syn: repetition. (***)
> The frequent *recurrence* of cancer even after it is seemingly cured makes it a particularly terrible disease.

36. Languid [lang-gwid]
adj syn: lacking energy; indifferent; slow. (**)
> The cat *languidly* cleaned its fur, ignoring the viciously snarling dog chained a few feet away.

37. Humane [hyoo-meyn]
adj syn: merciful; kindly.
> A *humane* man, the camp commander made sure to treat all the prisoners fairly.

38. Meager [mee-ger]
adj def: deficient in quantity or quality; scanty (**)
> Recently, an increasing number of employees have earned *meager* salaries from the company.

39. Illegible [ih-leg-i-ble]
adj syn: impossible or hard to read.
> This letter written by Tom was completely *illegible*.

40. Copious [koh-pee-uhs]
adj syn: abundant; plentiful.
> The hostess had prepared *copious* amounts of food for the banquet.

41. Amass [uh-mas]
verb syn: to collect into a mass or pile; to gather. (**)
> He *amassed* his papers for his memoirs.

42. Voluminous [vuh-**loo**-muh-nuhs]
adj syn: ample size; extent.
    Although it was a hot day, she was wearing a *voluminous* petticoat.

43. Embellish [em-**bel**-ish]
verb def: to enhance with fictitious addition. (**)
    Judy *embellished* herself with a lot of jewelry she had purchased at Macy's.

44. Purport [per-**pawart**]
verb syn: to confess; suppose; clean.
    Brad *purported* to be an opera lover, but he fell asleep at every performance he attended.

45. Dubious [**doo**-bee-uhs]
adj syn: doubtful; marked by or occasional doubt. (**)
    He made a *dubious* reply to her by email.

> **❝** *I was surprised to find so many words from this book appearing on the SAT test the last time I took it. I really want to recommend this book to anyone who is preparing for the SAT. This is a must-have book!* **❞**

Emily C (Queens of Peace High School)

Synonym

1. Speculative
   A) Plentiful
   B) Theoretical
   C) Barren
   D) Infertile
   E) Profit

2. Rigorous
   A) Redressing
   B) Flouting
   C) Sham
   D) Severe
   E) Fiasco

3. Purport
   A) Adulation
   B) Thwart
   C) Confess
   D) Prying
   E) Intrusion

4. Staunch
   A) Resolute
   B) Amend
   C) Approve
   D) Renewal
   E) Inadequacy

5. Coerced

    A) Rejection
    B) Ratification
    C) Compel
    D) Exemplary
    E) Laudatory

6. Supple

    A) Unethical
    B) Flexible
    C) Acclaimed
    D) Incisive
    E) Prosaic

7. Belabor

    A) Censure
    B) Liberal
    C) Conservative
    D) Unorthodox
    E) Scorn

8. Preclude

    A) Inhibit
    B) Futile
    C) Conjecture
    D) Betray
    E) Tribulation

Answer Keys

1) B 2) D 3) C 4) A 5) C 6) B 7) E 8) A

Antonym

1. Tame
A) Hapless
B) Obscure
C) Posthumously
D) Violent
E) Infamous

2. Adroit
A) Monastic
B) Premature
C) Abandon
D) Alter
E) Unskillful

3. Paucity
A) Acclaimed
B) Relinquish
C) Rich
D) Substitute
E) Supersede

4. Abase
A) Exalt
B) Clement
C) Stimulate
D) Appease
E) Inhibit

5. Rebut
A) Restrain
B) Obtain
C) Futile
D) Viable
E) Agree

6. Motley
  A) Nomadic
  B) Homogeneous
  C) Lugubrious
  D) Covetous
  E) Exotic

7. Copious
  A) Migrate
  E) Reprobate
  C) Insufficient
  D) Saunter
  E) Predator

8. Dubious
  A) Aloof
  B) Invoke
  C) Retrospect
  D) Certain
  E) Diffident

9. Meager
  A) Adequate
  B) Refractory
  C) Desultory
  D) Arcane
  E) Paragon

Answer Keys

1) D 2) E 3) C 4) A 5) E 6) B 7) C 8) D 9) A

1. **Rehabilitate** [ree-huh-**bil**-i-teyt]
   verb def: re-store to good health or condition. (**)
   > Susan checked herself into a clinic in order to *rehabilitate* herself from her drug addiction.

2. **Sporadic** [spuh-**rad**-ik]
   adj syn: infrequent; irregular. (****)
   > Since he followed the diet *sporadically*, Mick lapsed back into his old bad eating habits and did not lose weight.

3. **Gratuitous** [gruh-**too**-i-tuhs]
   adj syn: given freely or without cause. (**)
   > Since her opinion was not requested, her harsh criticism of his singing seemed like a *gratuitous* insult.

4. **Disillusion** [dis-i-**loo**-zhuhn]
   noun def: to free from or deprive of illusion.
   > Miraculously, his mind is beginning to be filled with *disillusions* he has never experienced before.

5. **Conflagration** [kon-fluh-**grey**-shuhn]
   noun syn: destructive fire. (*)
   > After the *conflagration* had finally died down, the city center was nothing but a mass of blackened ember.

6. **Concord** [kun-**kawrd**]
   noun syn: to agree.
   > The manager and her employees were in *concord* over the necessity of improving the product.

7. **Amalgamate** [uh-**mal**-guh-meyt]
   verb syn: to mix; to combine.
   > Giant industries *amalgamated* with Mega Products to form Giant-Mega Products Incorporated.

8. **Aberration** [ab-uh-**rey**-shuhn]
   noun def: something different from the usual. (**)
   > Due to the bizarre *aberrations* in the author's behavior, the
   > publicist decided that the less the public saw of her, the better.

9. **Analogous** [uh-**nal**-uh-guh]
   adj syn: comparable; similar; parallel. (***)
   > In a famous argument for the existence of God, the universe is
   > *analogous* to a mechanical watch, the creation of a divinely
   > intelligent "clockmaker."

10. **Surpass** [ser-**pas**]
    verb syn: to do better than, be superior to.
    > Ursula is a pretty girl, but her gorgeous sister *surpasses* her
    > in beauty.

11. **Resent** [ri-**zent**]
    verb syn: to feel or show displeasure. (***)
    > Jason *resented* his friend's attitude towards his teacher in class.

12. **Deride** [dih-**rahyd**]
    verb syn: to scoff; ridicule; mock.
    > The awkward child was often *derided* by his "cooler" peers.

13. **Simulate** [**sim**-yuh-leyt]
    verb def: to create a simulation; to make a pretense.
    > He *simulated* the manners of rich.

14. **Patrician** [puh-**trish**-uhn]
    noun syn: aristocrate. (*)
    > Although he was born a pauper, Claudius hoped eventually
    > to acquire a *patrician* standing in society.

15. **Preamble** [**pree**-am-buhl]
    noun def: an introductory statement. syn: preface; prelude.
    > The *preamble* to the Constitution begins with the famous words,
    > "We the people of the United States of America."

16. **Chide** [chayhd]

 verb syn: to scold; express disapproval. (**)

 Florence *chided* her poodle for eating the birthday cake she had baked for her birthday.

17. **Fraction** [**frak**-shuhn]

 noun def: a part as distinct from the whole of anything.

 The meeting started with a *fraction* of us present.

18. **Stalk** [stawk]

 verb syn: to hunt; pursue.

 The rock star put a restraining order on the insane woman who had *stalked* him for many years.

19. **Probe** [prohb]

 verb def: to search into or exam thoroughly.

 Sam has been trying to *probe* his conscience.

20. **Resuscitate** [ri-**suhs**-i-teyt]

 verb syn: to revive; to bring back to life. (***)

 The doctor managed to *resuscitate* the heart attack victim one minute after he had stopped breathing.

21. **Vicious** [**vish**-uhs]

 adj def: addicted to or characterized by vice; grossly immoral. spiteful, malicious. (**)

 Tom had been victimized by *vicious* gossips before he entered college.

22. **Insolence** [**in**-suh-luhus]

 noun def: an attitude or behavior that is bold and disrespectful. (*)

 Some feel that news reporters who shout questions at the president are behaving with *insolence*

23. Substantiate [suhb-**tan**-shee-yet]
verb syn: verified or supported by evidence. (***)
> The charge that Nixon had helped to cover up crimes was *substantiated* by his comments about it on a series of audiotapes.

24. Belie [bih-**lahy**]
verb def: to present a false or contradictory appearance.
> Julie's youthful appearance *belies* her long, distinguished career in show business.

25. Retract [ri-**trakt**]
verb syn: to draw in or take back.
> After Lance had *retracted* his insulting defeat, the troops retrenched back at the base to decide what to do next.

26. Salutation [sal-luy-**tey**-shuhn]
noun syn: greeting.
> Many people keep in touch by changing Christmas *salutations* once a year.

27. Alleviate [uh-**lee**-vee-yet]
verb def: to make lighter or more bearable. (***)
> Although no cure for AIDS has been found, doctors are able to *alleviate* the suffering of those with the disease.

28. Augment [**awg**-ment]
verb syn: to increase; expand; extend. (*)
> Ben *augmented* his salary with overtime hours as much as possible.

29. Entourage [ahn-too-**rahzh**]
noun def: a group of attendants or associates.
> The opera singer traveled with an *entourage* of 20 people.

30. Debacle [dey-**bah**-kuhl]
noun def: a general breakup or dispersion.
> The revolution ended in a *debacle*.

31. **Pertain** [per-**teyn**]
    verb syn: to have reference or relation; relate.
    The documents seemed to be *pertaining* to the lawsuit.

32. **Coalesce** [koh-uh-**les**]
    verb def: to grow together or cause to unite as one. (**)
    The different fraction of organization *coalesced* to form one united front against their opponents.

33. **Affable** [**af**-uh-buhl]
    adj syn: friendly; easy to approach. (*)
    The *affable* postman was on good terms with everyone on his route.

34. **Equanimity** [ee-kwuh-**nim**-i-tee]
    noun syn: calmness; composure.
    Kelly took the news that she had been fired with outward *equanimity* but she was in fact, crying inside.

35. **Resilient** [ri-**zil**-yuhnt]
    adj def: able to recover from difficulty.
    A professional athlete must be *resilient*, able to lose a game one day and come back the next with confidence and enthusiasm.

36. **Truculent** [**truhk**-yuh-luhnt]
    adj syn: aggressive; hostile; belligerent. (*)
    Hitler's *truculent* behavior in demanding more territory for Germany made it clear that war was inevitable.

37. **Abstruse** [ab-**stroos**]
    adj def: difficult to understand. (**)
    The philosopher's elucidation was so clear that he turned an *abstruse* subject into one his audience could grasp.

38. **Arcane** [ahr-**keyn**]
    adj syn: little-known; mysterious; obscure. (***)
    Eliot's "Waste Land" is filled with *arcane* lore, including quotations in Latin, Greek, French, German, and Sanskrit.

39. Unequivocal [uhn-**kwiv**-uh-kuhl]
adj syn: absolute; certain.
The Jury's verdict was *unequivocal*; the sadistic murderer would be locked up for life.

40. Esoteric [es-uh-**ter**-ik]
adj def: understood by only a learned few. (**)
Only a handful of experts are knowledgeable about the *esoteric* world of particular physics.

41. Impenetrable [im-**pen**-i-truth-buhl]
adj def: incapable of being understood, inscrutable; unfathomable. (***)
He tried to figure out an *impenetrable* mystery.

42. Grating [**grey**-ting]
adj verb def: to have an irritating or unpleasant.
His constant chatter *grates* on my nerves.

43. Sentimental [sen-tuh-**men**-tl]
adj def: pertaining to or dependent on sentiment.
We kept the old photograph for purely *sentimental* reasons.

44. Stilted [**stil**-tid]
adj syn: stifle; unnatural. (**)
The nervous father of the bride gave a rather *stilted* speech at the wedding banquet.

45. Havoc [**hav**-uhk]
noun syn: great destruction; devastation. (*)
The fire *havocked* throughout the house.

Synonym

1. Sporadic
      A) Insignificant
      B) Infrequent
      C) Dubious
      D) Coercive
      E) Repugnant

2. Disillusion
      A) Disenthrall
      B) Utopian
      C) Mawkish
      D) Venerable
      E) Surreptitious

3. Concord
      A) Awkward
      B) Haughty
      C) Decorous
      D) Disagree
      E) Optimistic

4. Aberration
      A) Antagonistic
      B) Candid
      C) Pompous
      D) Effusive
      E) Abnormal

5. Surpass
  A) Laconic
  B) Inscrutable
  C) Exceed
  D) Lyrical
  E) Euphonious

6. Preamble
  A) Avaricious
  B) Confer
  C) Prodigal
  D) Reside
  E) Prelude

7. Stalk
  A) Lachrymose
  B) Chase
  C) Extraneous
  D) Lethargy
  E) Regimen

8. Impenetrable
  A) Impassable
  B) Ostentatious
  C) Convoluted
  D) Transcend
  E) Fallacy

Answer keys

1) B 2) A 3) D 4) E 5) C 6) E 7) B 8) A

Antonym

1. Resuscitation
A) Enervate
B) Pursuit
C) Commitment
D) Mercenary
E) Agnostic

2. Insolence
A) Curmudgeon
B) Modest
C) Benefactor
D) Harbinger
E) Relic

3. Belie
A) Notion
B) Memento
C) Amorous
D) Attest
E) Bequeath

4. Alleviate
A) Appreciative
B) Subvert
C) Aggravate
D) Proscribe
E) Deprecate

5. Debacle
A) Cognizant
B) Relinquish
C) Lamentable
D) Flimsy
E) Boon

6. Coalesce
      A) Withstand
      B) Divide
      C) Sophisticated
      D) Detect
      E) Sturdy

7. Resilient
      A) Stubborn
      B) Amorphous
      C) Preeminent
      D) Impenetrable
      E) Viscous

8. Resent
      A) Vapid
      B) Regime
      C) Furtive
      D) Like
      E) Vapid

9. Augment
      A) Thwart
      B) Debase
      C) Abate
      D) Baleful
      E) Degrade

Answer Keys

1) A 2) B 3) D 4) C 5) E 6) B 7) A 8) D 9) E

1. **Snide** [snahyd]
   adj def: derogatory in a nasty or insinuating manner. (**)
   Paul made a *snide* remark about his boss.

2. **Presumptuous** [pri-**zuhmp**-choo-uhs]
   adj def: going beyond the limits of courtesy or appropriateness. (****)
   The senator winced when the *presumptuous* young staffer addressed him as "Chuck."

3. **Pedagogue** [**ped**-uh-gog]
   noun syn: teacher.
   Ghandi was regarded as an influential *pedagogue* in his society.

4. **Restitution** [res-ti-**too**-shuhn]
   adj def: arranged in or having the appearance of a mosaic
   The tessellated output of the correction volumes combines a set of sub-regions into one global correction set.

5. **Tessellated** [**tes**-uh-ley-tid]
   adj def: a form of government in which all power is vested in a few persons
   The *tessellated* output of the correction volumes combines a set of sub-regions into one global correction set.

6. **Dismay** [dis-**mey**]
   verb def: to break down the courage of completely, as by sudden attack. (*)
   The surprise attack *dismayed* the enemy.

7. **Sunder** [**suhn**-der]
   verb def: to separate; part; drive; sever
   During the cold war, an impenetrable wall *sundered* East and West Berlin.

8. **Suborn** [suh-**bawrn**]
   verb def: to bribe or induce
   Drug-trafficking revenues exacerbated corruption by enabling trafficking organizations to *suborn* government officials.

9. Mar [mahr]
verb syn: to damage; deface; spoil. (***)
Telephone poles *marred* the natural beauty of the countryside.

10. Offset [**awf**-set]
verb def: to counterbalance as an equivalent does; to compensate for.
The gains *offset* the losses.

11. Stoke [stohk]
verb def: to poke; stir up, and feed a fire
Size and success naturally *stoke* suspicion and cynicism.

12. Denounce [dih-**nouns**]
verb syn: to accuse; blame; decry. (**)
The advertising company was heavily *denounced* for the way it
depicted its female character.

13. Spurious [**spyoor**-ee-uhs]
adj syn: not genuine, or authentic. (***)
Quoting from a *spurious* bible, the cult leader declared that all
property should be signed over to him.

14. Opt [opt]
verb syn: to decide to leave or withdraw; to make a choice.
Jonathan *opted* out of the urban rat race and moved to
the countryside.

15. Shamble [**sham**-buhl]
verb def: to walk awkwardly with dragging feet
Disconsolate and exhausted after losing the match, the wrestler
shambled toward the locker room.

16. Supplant [suh-**plant**]
verb syn: replace; substitute; displace. (*)
After his miserable performance, a more experienced candidate
supplanted the raw young CEO.

17. Finagle [fi-**ney**-guhl]
verb syn: to trick; swindle; cheat. (*)
> A man *finagled* my best friend, Josh, out of two hundred dollars.

18. Winnow [**win**-oh]
verb syn: to drive; to blow away.
> John *winnowed* dirt on the floor by fanning.

19. Overhaul [oh-ver-**hawl**]
verb def: to investigate or examine thoroughly for repair or revision. (**)
> Next year we are going to *overhaul* the curriculum.

20. Grievous [**gree**-vuhs]
adj syn: causing grief or sorrow; serious and distressing.
> Maude and Bertha sobbed loudly throughout the *grievous* event.

21. Exult [ig-**zuhlt**]
verb syn: to rejoice; extreme happiness.
> The investor *exulted* as the price of the stocks he had bought skyrocketed.

22. Cabal [kuh-**bal**]
noun def: small group of secret plotters, as against government. (**)
> Steve established a *cabal* in order to overthrow the existing government.

23. Tawdry [**taw**-dree]
adj syn: gaudy; cheap; showy. (***)
> The performer changed into her *tawdry*, spangled costume and stepped out onto the stage to do her show.

24. Betray [bih-**trey**]
verb def: to deliver or expose to an enemy by treachery or disloyalty.
> Benedict Arnold *betrayed* his country.

25. Unremitting [uhn-ri-**mit**-ing]
  adj syn: not slackening or abating; incessant. (****)
  Paul made an *unremitting* attention to Jessica.

26. Condescending [kon-duh-**sen**-ding]
  adj def: having an attitude of superiority toward another,
          syn: patronizing.(****)
  "What a cute little car!" she remarked in a *condescending* style.
  "I suppose it is the nicest one someone like you could afford!"

27. Rubric [**roo**-brik]
  noun def: a title, heading, direction, or the like in a manuscript
  The *rubrics* at the beginning of the chapters are intended to
  be humorous.

28. Pulchritude [**puhl**-krit-tood]
  noun def: physical beauty; comeliness
  I do not judges who have to select this year's Miss America from
  the collection of female *pulchritude*.

29. Prurient [**proo** r-ee-uh nt]
  adj def: having inclined to have, characterized by lascivious
  The book that William was reading appealed to the *prurient*
  curiosity of its readers.

30. Usher [**uhsh**-er]
  verb def: to act as an usher to; lead; introduce.
  She *ushered* them to their seats.

31. Lament [luh-**ment**]
  verb syn: to deplore; grieve.
  The children continued to *lament* the death of the goldfish weeks
  after its demise.

32. Osseous [**os**-ee-uh s]
  adj def: composed of, containing, or resembling bone; bony
  The hollow "soft spot" found that at the top of the infant's skull
  gradually closes as new *osseous* tissues fills in the gap.

33. Encroach [en-krohch]
verb def: to advance beyond proper, or established.

A dictatorship of the majority is *encroaching* on the rights of the individual.

34. Bypass [bahy-pas]
verb syn: to avoid.

def: to neglect to consult or to ignore the opinion.

Alex *bypassed* the foreman and took his grievance straight to the owner.

35. Rhetoric [ret-er-ik]
noun def: persuasive use of language. (***)

Lincoln's talent for *rhetoric* was evident in his beautifully expressed Gettysburg Address.

36. Surfeit [sur-fit]
noun syn: excessive amount; exceeded. (**)

Because of the *surfeit* of pigs, pork prices have never been lower.

37. Deficit [def-uh-sit]
noun syn: a disadvantage; impairment; handicap.

The team's major *deficit* is its poor pitching.

38. Juxtapose [juhk-stuh-pohz]
verb syn: to put side by side. (*)

It was strange to see the actor Charlton Hesston and musician Bob Dylan *juxtaposed* at the awards ceremony.

39. Phlegmatic [fleg-mat-ik]
adj def: sluggish and unemotional in temperament. (**)

It was surprising to see Tom, who in normally so *phlegmatic*, acting excited.

40. Interregnum [in-ter-**reg**-nuh m]
   noun def: an interval of time between the close of a sovereign's reign
   The democratic regime proved to be a short-lived *interregnum*
   between dictatorships.

41. Confront [kuhn-**fruhnt**]
   verb syn: to face in hostility or defiance; oppose.
   The feuding factions *confronted* one another.

42. Overwrought [oh-ver-**rawt**]
   adj def: extremely or excessively excited or agitated
   But in the experiment, readers judged the authors of the
   overwrought texts to be not-so-bright.

43. Compassionate [kuhm-**pash**-uh-nit]
   adj def: having or showing compassion; a compassionate person.
   The *compassionate* man saved a Jewish family during the Holocaust.

44. Vigilant [**vij**-uh-luhnt]
   adj syn: attentive; watchful. (**)
   Air traffic controllers must be *vigilant* in order to ensure that
   planes do not collide with one another.

45. Reputable [**rep**-yuh-tah-buhl]
   adj syn: having a great reputation; respect. (*)
   Dr. Kennedy made a *reputable* speech in front of his students.

Synonym

1. Presumptuous
- A) Projection
- B) Corroborate
- C) Arrogant
- D) Inspire
- E) Dexterous

2. Encroach
- A) Indefatigable
- B) Obsequious
- C) Syncopated
- D) Establish
- E) Transcendent

3. Exacerbate
- A) Worsen
- B) Bombastic
- C) Obscure
- D) Verbose
- E) Clarified

4. Mar
- A) Captivating
- B) Damage
- C) Defined
- D) Exuberant
- E) Misconstrue

5. Denounce

 A) Candor
 B) Humility
 C) Innuendo
 D) Farce
 E) Criticize

6. Offset

 A) Monotony
 B) Compensate
 C) Prudence
 D) Replicating
 E) Displacing

7. Supplant

 A) Vague
 B) Demonstrating
 C) Conciliatory
 D) Timorous
 E) Replace

8. Vigilant

 A) Attentive
 B) Disparage
 C) Scarcity
 D) Implement
 E) Vengeance

Answer Keys

1) C   2) D   3) A   4) B   5) E   6) B   7) E   8) A

Antonym

1. Exult
   A) Grieve
   B) Forbid
   C) Surpass
   D) Confront
   E) Provincial

2. Tawdry
   A) Indigenous
   B) Descendant
   C) Sophisticated
   D) Benign
   E) Abstract

3. Betray
   A) Lessen
   B) Injustice
   C) Landlord
   D) Faithful
   E) Magnified

4. Condescending
   A) Exploitation
   B) Humble
   C) Aggressive
   D) Delighted
   E) Impulsive

5. Unequivocal
   A) Warily
   B) Shrewd
   C) Enthralled
   D) Alarm
   E) Ambiguous

6. Lament

    A) Repeal
    B) Rejoice
    C) Expatriate
    D) Forbid
    E) Prompt

7. Surfeit

    A) Compiled
    B) Reticent
    C) Vexed
    D) Indulgent
    E) Lack

8. Spurious

    A) Genuine
    B) Gauche
    C) Sanguine
    D) Perplex
    E) Virulent

9. Snide

    A) Subterfuge
    D) Disdain
    C) Baleful
    D) Xenophobia
    E) Lofty

Answer keys

1) A 2) C 3) D 4) B 5) E 6) B 7) E 8) A 9) E

1. **Penurious** [puh-**noor**-ee-uhs]
   adj syn: extremely frugal; stingy; curmudgeon.
   > Haunted by memories of poverty, he lived in a *penurious* fashion, driving a twelve-year-old car and wearing only the cheapest clothes.

2. **Frugal** [**froo**-guhl]
   adj syn: spending little; thrifty. (***)
   > With our last few dollars, we bought a *frugal* dinner: a loaf of bread and a piece of cheese.

3. **Gallop** [**gal**-uhp]
   verb def: to ride a horse at a gallop; ride at full speed.
   > Paul and Tim *galloped* off to meet their friends.

4. **Embitter** [em-**bit**-er]
   verb def: cause to feel bitterness. (*)
   > Failure has *embittered* him.

5. **Mortify** [**mawr**-tuh-fehy]
   verb syn: to humiliate or shame, as by injury to one's pride. (**)
   > Mr. Han felt *mortified* by John who called him a loser.

6. **Thereafter** [thair-**af**-ter]
   adverb syn: after that in time; sequence.
   > *Thereafter,* they did not speak.

7. **Transcend** [tran-**send**]
   verb syn: superior; surpass; excel. (**)
   > His competitiveness made him want to *transcend.*

8. **Fallacy** [**fal**-uh-see]
   noun syn: a deceptive; misleading; false notion. (***)
   > The idea that the world is flat was popular *fallacy.*

9. **Distort** [dis-**stawrt**]
   verb def: twist awry or out of shape.
   Arthritis had *distorted* his fingers.

10. **Abash** [uh-**bash**]
    verb def: to destroy the self-confidence. (**)
    Jonathan *abashed* Susan by sneering.

11. **Veil** [veyl]
    verb syn: to cover or conceal with something.
    She *veiled* her face in black.
    A heavy fog *veiled* the shoreline.

12. **Taciturn** [**tas**-i-turn]
    adj def: inclined to silence; reserved in speech. (**)
    The clerk's *taciturn* nature earned him the nickname
    "Silent Sammy."

13. **Utter** [**uht**-er]
    verb syn: speak; pronounce.
    Words were *uttered* in my hearing.

14. **Brood** [brood]
    verb syn: to think or worry persistently or moodily. (**)
    Joseph *brooded* the problems he faced.

15. **Paralyze** [**par**-uh-lahyz]
    verb syn: inactivity; inability.
    The strike *paralyzed* communications in a small town.

16. **Ancillary** [**an**-suh-ler-ee]
    noun syn: subordinate; subsidiary; assisting.
    Slides, records, and other *ancillaries* can be used with the basic
    textbooks.

17. Taxonomy [tak-**son**-uh-mee]
noun def: science of classification.

> Certain strange species do not seem to fit into the systems of classification used in traditional *taxonomy*.

18. Synthesis [**sin**-thuh-sis]
noun syn: blend; combination. (**)

> The methods used in the experiment were a *synthesis* of techniques taken from biology and medicine.

19. Antagonist [an-**tag**-uh-nist]
noun syn: foe; opponent; adversary.

> The child and cat became bitter *antagonists* after the child pulled the cat's tail.

20. Accost [uh-**kawst**]
verb syn: approach, especially with a greeting.

> The beggar *accosted* me for money.

21. Enlighten [en-**lahyt**-n]
verb syn: to give intellectual or spiritual light to. (**)

> We hope the results of our research will *enlighten* our colleagues.

22. Convene [kuhn-**veen**]
verb syn: to meet; to come together; to assemble.

> The members of the board usually *convene* at least once a week.

23. Eradicate [ih-**rad**-i-keyt]
verb syn: to erase or to wipe out.

> Although the general standard of living has significantly improved in recent decades, it is unlikely that poverty will ever be completely *eradicated* in this country.

24. Tangential [tan-**jen**-shuhl]
adj syn: digressing; diverting. (***)

> Your argument is interesting, but it is *tangential* to the matter at hand, so I suggest we get back to the point.

25. Discern [dis-**surn**]
verb def: to perceive something obscure. (**)
> It is easy to *discern* the difference between real butter and butter-flavored topping.

26. Culmination [kuhl-muh-**ney**-shuhn]
noun syn: climax; final stage. (*)
> Fireworks marked the *culmination* of the festivities.

27. Exorbitant [ig-**zawr**-bi-tuhnt]
adj syn: extravagant; greater than reasonable.
> The harvest was destroyed by *exorbitantly* freezing temperatures.

28. Suppress [suh-**pres**]
verb def: put an end to the activities to.
> The government decided to *suppress* the Communist party.

29. Affidavit [afi-**dey**-vit]
noun def: a written declaration upon oath made before an authorized official
> We have a signed *affidavit* stating that the two men were seen entering the building.

30. Amnesia [am-**nee**-zhuh]
noun def: loss of a large block of interrelated memories
> The science behind that kind of *amnesia* remains murky, because such intense fear is a state as yet inaccessible to science.

31. Rouse [rouz]
verb def: to bring out of a state of sleep.
> Brian was *roused* to action by courageous words.

32. Wrath [rawth]
noun syn: extreme anger; ire; fury; rage.
> He denounced the criminals in a speech filled with righteous *wrath*.

33. Betoken [bih-toh-kuh-n]
verb def: to give evidence of; indicate

The appearance of those who had been in consultation did not *betoken* a hopeful prospect for impeachment.

34. Solace [sol-is]
noun syn: comfort in distress; consolation. (*)

Upsets as she was by her poodle's death, Florence took *solace* in the fact he had died happy.

35. Inevitable [in-ev-i-tuh-buhl]
adj syn: certain; unavoidable. (**)

"The value of this acquisition to our company is *inevitable*," bragged the CEO.

36. Mitigate [mit-i-geyt]
verb syn: to make less severe; to relieve. (***)

Wallace certainly committed the assault, but the verbal abuse he had received helps to explain his behavior and somewhat *mitigates* his guilt.

37. Squelch [skwelch]
verb syn: to put down; suppress; silence. (*)

The police made a continuous effort to *squelch* the rebellions creating numerous problems.

38. Alacrity [uh-lak-ri-tee]
noun syn: promptness; speed.

Thrilled with the job offer, he accepted with *alacrity*- "Before they change their minds!" he thought.

39. Recriminate [ri-krim-uh-neyt]
verb syn: to accuse, often in response to an accusation. (**)

Divorce proceedings sometimes become bitter, as the two parties *recriminate* each other over the causes of the breakup.

40. Affected [uh-fek-tid]
adj syn: influenced.

Dan was deeply *affected* by Jason's generosity.

41. Avow [uh-vou]

verb syn: to declare frankly or openly. (**)

Peter *avowed* himself an opponent of all alliances.

42. Exacerbate [ig-zas-er-beyt]

verb syn: to make worse or more severe. (***)

The roads in our town already have too much traffic; building a new shopping mall will *exacerbate* the problem.

43. Delineate [dih-lin-ee-yet]

verb syn: to outline; to describe. (**)

Naturalists had long suspected the fact of evolution, but Darwin was the first to *delineate* a process, natural selection, through which evolution could occur.

44. Exotic [ig-zot-ik]

adj syn: foreign; romantic; strange.

The atmosphere of the restaurant was *exotic*, but the food was ordinary.

45. Tirade [tahy-reyd]

noun def: extended scolding. syn: denunciation; harangue. (**)

The cigar smoker went into a bitter *tirade* denouncing the antismoking forces that had succeeded in banning smoking from most planes and restaurants.

> **"** Mastering the Core SAT Words with William Shin *is by far the most reliable source out there. It carefully guides you through each and every word and supports your progress towards the 800 in Critical Reading and Writing. Truly profound.* **"**

Victor *(Paramus High School)*

Synonym

1. Penurious
      A) Parsimonious
      B) Repulse
      C) Placid
      D) Irritated
      E) Curt

2. Mortify
      A) Incensed
      B) Droll
      C) Perturbed
      D) Embarrass
      E) Amiable

3. Fallacy
      A) Weakened
      B) Sullen
      C) Misconception
      D) Inopportune
      E) Meager

4. Veil
      A) Auspicious
      B) Cover
      C) Modest
      D) Bustling
      E) Manufactured

5. Taciturn
> A) Rural
> B) Seedy
> C) Deserted
> D) Feigned
> E) Reticent

6. Brood
> A) Envision
> B) Divulge
> C) Scantier
> D) Keener
> E) Ponder

7. Convene
> A) Perceived
> B) Frown upon
> C) Exemption
> D) Assemble
> E) Relish

8. Penurious
> A) Poverty
> B) Lethargic
> C) Scourge
> D) Champion
> E) Incarcerate

Answer keys

1) A 2) D 3) C 4) B 5) E 6) E 7) D 8) A

Antonym

1. Avow
  A) Addendum
  B) Censure
  C) Rail at
  D) Malicious
  E) Compromise

2., Discern
  A) Abolish
  B) Wistful
  C) Grudge
  D) Neglect
  E) Abide

3. Squelch
  A) Cynic
  B) Dilution
  C) Aid
  D) Neglect
  E) Reign

4. Solace
  A) Misnomer
  B) Retelling
  C) Barren
  D) Fault
  E) Discomfort

5. Inevitable
  A) Avoidable
  B) Subtle
  C) Assault
  D) Titillates
  E) Delve

6. Alacrity
    A) Metes
    B) Dullness
    C) Hinge on
    D) Spurn
    E) Condone

7. Exotic
    A) Ordinary
    B) Discreet
    C) Intriguing
    D) Reflect
    E) Thwart

8. Tirade
    A) Abuse
    B) Disaffected
    C) Aesthetic
    D) Improvident
    E) Harmony

9. Culmination
    A) Acme
    B) Obstinate
    C) Beginning
    D) Valor
    E) Inert

Answer Keys

1) B 2) D 3) C 4) E 5) A 6) B 7) A 8) E 9) C

1. ## Whimsical [hwim-zi-kuhl]
   adj syn: unpredictable; capricious; changeable. (***)
   > The pop star has changed her image so many times that each new transformation now appears *whimsical* rather than purposeful.

2. ## Barefaced [bair-feyst]
   adj syn: shameless; impudent; audacious
   > The *barefaced* cheek of the question sucked all the breath from Jeffrey.

3. ## Pragmatism [prag-mat-ik]
   noun def: a belief in approaching problems through practical rather than theoretical means.
   > Roosevelt's approach toward the Great Depression was based on *pragmatism*: "Try something." He said; "If it doesn't work, try something else."

4. ## Outstrip [out-strip]
   verb syn: to surpass; to excel.
   > A car can *outstrip* the local train.

5. ## Aggrandize [uh-gran-dahyz]
   verb def: to make larger or greater in power. (**)
   > The entire millionaire really wanted was to *aggrandize* his personal wealth as much as possible.

6. ## Bedraggle [bih-drag-uh-l]
   verb def: to make limp and soiled, as with rain or dirt
   > Veronica was so *bedraggled* by the relentless rain that she couldn't wait to get into some dry clothes.

7. ## Artificial [ahr-tuh-fish-uhl]
   adj syn: fake; simulated; shame.
   > He is allergic to the *artificial* vanilla flavoring.

8. **Garish** [**gair**-ish]
   adj syn: excessively bright; glaring. (**))
   Sophia sometimes surprises her friends by wearing a *garish* hat.

9. **Bisect** [bahy-**sekt**]
   verb syn: to cut into two. (***)
   Tom accidentally found the spot where the railroad tracks *bisected* the highway.

10. **Acumen** [uh-**kyoo**-muhn]
    noun syn: sharpness of insight.
    The portfolio manager's financial *acumen* helped him select high-yield stocks for his clients.

11. **Flout** [flout]
    verb syn: to treat contemptuously; to scorn. (*)
    Despite repeated warnings, Peter and Joe have continued to *flout* the traffic regulation.

12. **Defiance** [dih-**fahy**-uhns]
    noun syn: open disregard; contempt.
    Any *defiance* of the authoritarian regime would have dire consequence.

13. **Scrutiny** [**skroot**-n-ee]
    noun def: careful observation. (**))
    The prehistoric fossils were given careful *scrutiny* by a team of scientists.

14. **Raze** [reyz]
    verb syn: to tear down; demolish.
    The house had been *razed*: there was nothing left but splinters and bricks.

15. **Derelict** [**der**-uh-likt]
   adj syn: neglectful of duty; delinquent.
      A great amount of treasure was found in a *derelict* ship in the middle of ocean.

16. **Grimy** [**grahy**-mee]
   adj syn: dirty; filthy.
      Beth was displeased when her date, Spike, showed up in a *grimy* T-shirt.

17. **Complement** [**kom**-pluh-muhnt]
   noun def: something that completes or makes perfect. (**)
      A good wine is a *complement* to a good meal.

18. **Tremulous** [**trem**-yuh-luhs]
   adj syn: trembling; quivering; fearful; timid.
      The *tremulous* stray cat hardly dared to approach the bowl of milk the boy offered.

19. **Lithe** [lahyth]
   adj syn: flexible; graceful. (***)
      The ballet dancer was almost *lithe* as an elegant bird.

20. **Fickle** [**fik**-uhl]
   adj def: likely to change.
      Many people in the island are getting tired of the *fickle* weather.

21. **Reprise** [ri-**prahyz**]
   noun syn: repetition. (****)
      The soloist ended her aria with a *reprise* of its beautiful refrain.

22. **Infuse** [in-**fyooz**]
   verb syn: to introduce.
      The energetic new principal *infused* new life into the school.

23. Procure [proh-**kyoor**]
verb syn: to obtain or get by care. (*)
> Bob was trying to *procure* secret document in order to sell to
> the enemy.

24. Diverge [dih-**verj**]
verb def: to move in different direction. (*)
> Frost's poem "The road Less Travel" tells of the choice he made
> when "Two roads *diverged* in a yellow wood."

25. Confine [kuhn-**fahyn**]
verb def: to enclose within bounds.
> She *confined* her remarks to error in the report.
> He *confined* his efforts to finish the book.

26. Drench [drench]
verb syn: to cover or fill completely.
> The trees in tropical forests are *drenched* with sunlight.

27. Susceptible [suh-**sep**-tuh-buhl]
adj syn: defenseless; unprotected; innocent; vulnerable. (**)
> The child whisked the *susceptible* little duckling out of the raging
> whirlpool just in time.

28. Squander [**skwon**-der]
verb syn: to use up carelessly; to waste. (**)
> Those who made donations to the charity were outraged to learn
> that its director had *squandered* millions on fancy dinners
> and first-class travel.

29. Liable [**lahy**-uh-buhl]
adj syn: legally responsible.
> You are *liable* for the damage caused by your action.

30. Immune [ih-**myoon**]
adj syn: to exempt; to protect from harm or disease.
> After you get chicken pox once, you are *immune* to the disease.

31. Credulity [kruh-**doo**-li-tee]
noun def: willingness to believe even with little evidence. (**)
> Con artists fool people by taking advantage of their *credulity*.

32. Morbid [**mawr**-bid]
adj syn: gruesome; gloomy. (*)
> Mrs. Fletcher had a *morbid* fascination with her dead daughter, displaying photos of her everywhere.

33. Foster [**faw**-ster]
verb syn: to nourish; cultivate.
> The record agent *fostered* the development of his clients by sending them a variety of brochures.

34. Abate [uh-**beyt**]
verb syn: to decrease; to reduce. (**)
> As the hurricane's force *abated*, the winds dropped and the sea became calm.

35. Flourish [**flur**-ish]
verb def: to make dramatic, sweeping gestures.
> Unexpectedly regional markets have *flourished* in recent years.

36. Innocuous [ih-**nok**-yoo-uhs]
adj syn: harmless; inoffensive.
> I was surprised that Andrea took offense at such as *innocuous* joke.

37. Prevalent [**prev**-a-lent]
adj syn: widespread
> The teacher struggled to counteract the *prevalent* belief in the school that girls could give boy cookies.

38. Indomitable [in-**dom**-i-tuh-buhl]
adj syn: fearless; unconquerable.
> Samson was *indomitable* in battle until the treacherous Delia cut off his hairs, taking away his strength.

39. Expeditious [ek-spi-**dish**-uhs]
adj syn: promptness.
> Lim made an *expeditious* answer to his teacher's inquiry.

40. Astute [uh-**stoot**]
adj syn: observant; intelligent. (**)
> Alan's years of experience in Washington and his personal acquaintance with many political insiders make him an *astute* commentator on politics.

41. Compelling [kuhm-**pel**-ing]
adj def: having a powerful effect. (***)
> The defense lawyer's *compelling* arguments made the jurors sympathize with the cold-blooded killer.

42. Obligate [**ob**-li-geyt]
verb def: to bind or oblige morally or legally.
> She *obliged* her husband to purchase a building.

43. Insolent [in-**suh**-luhnt]
adj syn: rude; arrogant. (**)
> "How dare you, *insolent* wretch!" roared the king when the peasant laughed at the sight of him stumbling into the mud.

44. Premonition [pree-muh-**nish**-uhn]
noun def: a feeling of anticipation of or anxiety over a future event.
> Dr. Schmidt had a vague *premonition* of danger.

45. Fraudulent [**fraw**-juh-luhnt]
adj syn: deceitful; dishonest. (**)
> The factory engaged in *fraudulent* practices, producing radios with defected components.

Synonym

1. Morbid
- A) Gloomy
- B) Progenitor
- C) Hybrid
- D) Descendants
- E) Conglomeration

2. Aggrandize
- A) Spores
- B) Convincing
- C) Bigger
- D) Inept
- E) Liability

3. Garish
- A) Sarcastic
- B) Rejoinder
- C) Venerate
- D) Flashy
- E) Bully

4. Acumen
- A) Coax
- B) Subsidizing
- C) Donate
- D) Shrewdness
- E) Elicit

5. Defiance

    A) Transmit

    B) Disregard

    C) Ceased

    D) Ceded

    E) Pyromaniac

6. Raze

    A) Accomplice

    B) Consequence

    C) Premonition

    D) Arsonist

    E) Destroy

7. Grimy

    A) Assortment

    B) Ungainly

    C) Rampant

    D) Unvarying

    E) Filthy

8. Whimsical

    A) Caprice

    B) Abhor

    C) Berate

    D) Candid

    E) Elude

Answer Keys

1) A 2) C 3) D 4) D 5) B 6) E 7) E 8) A

Antonym

1. Tremulous
    A) Brave
    B) Undertook
    C) Procure
    D) Entreat
    E) Precipitate

2. Fickle
    A) Merged
    B) Faithful
    C) Evolved
    D) Barged
    E) Beguile

3. Procure
    A) Obtain
    B) Salvaged
    C) Concession
    D) Interruption
    E) Lose

4. Confine
    A) Legislated
    B) Deem
    C) Free
    D) Restrict
    E) Indict

5. Squander
    A) Excommunicate
    B) Rally
    C) Spawn
    D) Frugal
    E) Immoral

6. Abate

A) Amplify
B) Blister
C) Wrecked
D) Negotiate
E) Balk

7. Insolent

A) Bargain
B) Rude
C) Flounder
D) Recoil
E) Reconsider

8. Astute

A) Adroit
B) Belie
C) Attest
D) Forte
E) Asinine

9. Susceptible

A) Rehabilitate
B) Sporadic
C) Resist
D) Mock
E) Lavish

Answer keys

1) A 2) B 3) E 4) C 5) D 6) A 7) B 8) E 9) C

1. Speculative [spek-yuh-ley-tiv]

adj syn: involving assumption; uncertain. (***)

The theories I'm presenting are purely *speculative*, and they shouldn't be acted upon until more research has been done to test them out.

2. Subordinate [suh-bawr-din-it]

verb syn: to make secondary; absolute obey.

It is a fact that more power nations often *subordinate* weaker ones.

3. Manipulative [muh-nip-yuh-ley-tiv]

verb syn: to manage; to influence.

Crystal always seems to *manipulate* her friends' feelings.

4. Obstinate [ob-stuh-nit]

adj syn: persistent; unyielding.

Senator, Kennedy, appeared to be an *obstinate* advocacy of high tariffs.

5. Impetuous [im-pech-oo-uhs]

adj syn: stimulous; impulsive.

Tim usually tries not to make an *impetuous* decision.

The grant for building <u>The Opera House</u> gave *impetuous* to the city's cultural life.

6. Valor [val-er]

noun syn: boldness; determination. (*)

During World War Two, Otis received a medal of *valor* from the president of the United States.

7. Agonize [ag-uh-nahyz]

verb syn: to suffer extreme pain; anguish.

He *agonized* to suffer for a prize.

8. **Culmination** [kuhl-nuh-**mey**-shuhn]
   noun syn: climax; final stage. (***)
   Fireworks marked the *culmination* of the festivities.

9. **Distress** [dih-**stres**]
   verb def: to compel by pain; to force of circumstances.
   His suffering *distressed* him into committing suicide.

10. **Nexus** [**nek**-suhs]
    noun def: a means of connection; tie; link.
    Michael played a crucial role as a *nexus* of communication between the two groups.

11. **Phenomena** [fi-**noh**-uh-nuh]
    noun syn: a fact; occurrence; circumstance.
    Daniel has spent numerous hours studying the *phenomena* of nature.

12. **Vicissitude** [vi-**sis**-tood]
    noun syn: change; variation; ups and downs. (***)
    Investors must be prepared for *vicissitudes* in the market and learn not to panic when stock prices fall occasionally.

13. **Juncture** [**juhngk**-cher]
    noun def: a point of time.
    At this *juncture,* we must decide whether to stay or to walk out.

14. **Conjecture** [kuhn-**jek**-cher]
    noun syn: speculation; prediction. (**)
    The actor refused to comment, forcing gossip columnists to make *conjectures* on his love life.

15. **Inquiry** [in-**kwahyr**-ee]
    noun def: a seeking or requesting for truth.
    An FBI agent made a number of *inquiries* to the suspect in order to find out a substantial evidence to arrest him.

16. Vulgar   [vuhl-ger]

adj syn: indecent; obscene; lewd.

His recently released *vulgar* painting disgraced his reputation he had established for the last twenty years.

17. Divisive   [dih-vahy-siv]

adj syn: creating disunity or conflict. (*)

The leader used *divisive* tactics to put his enemies against each other.

18. Decline   [dih-klahyn]

verb syn: to withhold; deny consent.

He *declined* to say more about it

19. Sedentary   [sed-n-ter-ee]

adj syn: inactive; stationary; sluggish. (**)

Americans, who often work in *sedentary* office jobs, are becoming more overweight and out of shape.

20. Sordid   [sawr-did]

adj syn: filthy; contemptible; corrupt.

The details of the president's affair were so *sordid* that many people were too disgusted to read them.

21. Refute   [ri-fyoot]

verb syn: to contradict; discredit. (*)

The president managed to *refute* the charges against him.

22. Disclaim   [dis-kleym]

verb syn: deny; disown; repudiate.

Stephen *disclaimed* the marriage rumor circulating in the press.

23. Stipulate   [stip-yuh-leyt]

verb syn: to specify; to require. (**)

Total disarmament was *stipulated* in the peace treaty.

24. Scrupulous [**skroo**-pyuh-luhs]
adj syn: honest; careful; precise. (***)

David could not have stolen Carmen's money; he is too *scrupulous* to do such as thing.

25. Impulsive [im-**puhl**-siv]
adj syn: spontaneous; unpredictable.

Sarah made an *impulsive* decision to purchase a dress that she couldn't afford.

26. Circumscribe [**sur**-kuhm-skrahyb]
verb def: to define by a limit; boundary.

Originally, the role of the executive branch of government was clearly *circumscribed*, but that role has greatly expanded over time.

27. Irreverent [ih-**rev**-er-uhnt]
adj syn: disrespectful; gently; humorously mocking. (**)

Kevin's *irreverent* attitude in Sunday school annoyed the priest, but amused the other children.

28. Corroborating [kuh-**rob**-uh-reyt]
adj syn: supporting with evidence; confirming. (***)

A passerby who had witnessed the crime gave *corroborating* testimony about the presence of the accused person.

29. Extant [ek-**stuhnt**]
adj syn: currently in existence.

Of the seven ancient "Wonders of the World," only the pyramids of Egypt are still *extant*.

30. Dwindle [**dwin**-dl]
verb def: to become smaller and smaller; shrink. (*)

His vast fortune has *dwindled* away.

31. Thrive [thrahyv]
verb syn: to grow; to develop.

The children *thrived* in the country.

32. Officious [uh-**fish**-uhs]

adj syn: too helpful; meddlesome.

The *officious* waiter butted into the couples' conversation, advising them on how to take out a mortgage.

33. Rancorous [**rang**-ker-uhs]

adj syn: expressing bitter hostility. (**)

Many Americans are disgusted by recent political campaign, which seem more *rancorous* than ever before.

34. Punctilious [puhngk-**til**-ee-uhs]

adj def: very concerned about proper forms of behavior. (*)

A *punctilious* dresser like James would rather skip the party altogether than wear the wrong color tie.

35. Myopic [mahy-**op**-ik]

adj syn: nearsighted. (***)

The *myopic* old man needed a magnifying glass to read the morning paper.

36. Entreat [en-**treet**]

verb syn: to plead; beg.

I *entreated* him to just tell me what the problem was instead of booting it up inside, but he refused.

37. Deferential [def-uh-**ren**-shul]

adj def: respectful and polite in a submissive way. (**)

Unlike other people, Douglass had the *deferential* attitude toward someone who had been a servant his whole life.

38. Admonish [ad-**mon**-ish]

verb syn: to caution; to reprimand. (*)

My mother began to *admonish* me about my poor grade.

39. Confide [kuhn-**fahyd**]
verb def: to impart secrets truthfully; discuss private matter.
She *confides* in no one but her husband.

40. Wrath [rawth]
noun syn: strong; stern; fierce anger. (**)
Lim felt a *wrath* when he heard about the rumor that might dishonor his reputation.

41. Overlook [oh-ver-**look**]
verb syn: to disregard; to ignore; fail to notice. (*)
Only a parent could *overlook* that kind of behavior.

42. Fabricate [**fab**-ri-keyt]
verb syn: to make by art or skill and labor; construct.
The finest craftspeople are able to *fabricate* this clock.

43. Stint [stint]
verb def: to be sparing or frugal. (**)
Albert *stinted* for years in order to save money.

44. Plague [pleyg]
noun syn: widespread affliction; calamity.
It has generally been believed that a *plague* is regarded as a direct punishment by God.

45. Trifling [**trahy**-fling]
adj syn: of slight worth; trivial; trite; insignificant. (****)
That little glitch in the computer program is a *trifling* error; in general, it works really well.

Synonym

1. Speculative
A) Theoretical
B) Presumptuous
C) Dogmatic
D) Disarming
E) Patronize

2. Impetus
A) Epitaph
B) Belated
C) Stimulus
D) Antiquity
E) Voluble

3. Agonize
A) Insensitive
B) Pessimistic
C) Truculent
D) Suffer
E) Depressed

4. Phenomena
A) Plot
B) Silly
C) Gloomy
D) Mythical
E) Wonder

5. Vicissitude
A) Deficit
B) Change
C) Brink
D) Absorption
E) Absence

6. Conjecture
A) Noncommittal
B) Guess
C) Eradication
D) Incense
E) Mournful

7. Vulgar
A) Offensive
B) Distraught
C) Promiscuous
D) Genial
E) Famish

8. Obstinate
A) Regress
B) Moderate
C) Stubborn
D) Oppress
E) Tame

Answer keys

1) A   2) C   3) D   4) E   5) B   6) B   7) A   8) B

Antonym

1. Divisive
      A) Ghastly
      B) Intolerable
      C) Agree
      D) Pretentious
      E) Forlorn

2. Sedentary
      A) Infectious
      B) Stolid
      C) Patriarchal
      D) Rubrics
      E) Energetic

3. Stipulate
      A) Pseudonym
      B) Criteria
      C) Imply
      D) Egregious
      E) Inedible

4. Scrupulous
      A) Negligent
      B) Sodden
      C) Monetary
      D) Mundane
      E) Replace

5. Irreverent
      A) Lofty
      B) Respect
      C) Vacillating
      D) Harass
      E) Plummet

6. Dwindle
A) Insinuate
B) Ravage
C) Flounder
D) Assault
E) Enlarge

7. Myopic
A) Tottering
B) Upbraid
C) Monitor
D) Far-sighted
E) Specify

8. Agonize
A) Afflict
B) Deplore
C) Not Worry
D) Matriculate
E) Lucid

9. Reluctant
A) Anxious
B) Affluent
C) Carp
D) Desecrate
E) Mollify

Answer keys

1) C 2) E 3) C 4) A 5) B 6) E 7) D 8) C 9) A

1. **Outwardly** [**out**-werd-lee]
   adverb def: toward the outside.
   > The pier stretched *outwardly* from the shore.

2. **Agitation** [aj-i-**tey**-shuhn]
   noun syn: commotion; excitement; uneasiness. (*)
   > The patient's *agitation* was obvious; she was terrified at
   > the thought of undergoing the operation.

3. **Furious** [**fyoor**-ee-uhs]
   adj def: fully violent passion, or rage.
   > He turned out to be *furious* about the accident.

4. **Apprehensive** [ap-ri-**hen**-siv]
   adj def: uneasy or fearful about something.
   > The government officers are seriously *apprehensive* for the safety of
   > the mountain climbers.

5. **Forthright** [**fawrth**-rahyt]
   adj syn: frank; going straight to the point.
   > It is sometimes difficult to be *forthright* and not give offense.

6. **Meticulous** [muh-**tik**-u-lous]
   adj def: talking or showing extreme care about details. (**)
   > Johnson has been known as a *meticulous* craftsman.

7. **Dilatory** [**dil**-uh-tawr-ee]
   adj syn: delaying; procrastinating.
   > The lawyer used various *dilatory* tactics, hoping that his opponent
   > would get tired of waiting for a trial and drop the case.

8. **Peevish** [**pee**-vish]
   adj syn: querulous; fretful; discontent.
   > Steve used to be known as an expert in dealing with a *peevish*
   > youngster.

9. **Inadequate** [in-**ad**-i-kwit]
   adj syn: not enough or sufficient.
   > Alex was extremely disappointed by the *inadequate* scholarship
   > provided by the university.

10. **Debilitate** [dih-**bil**-i-teyt]
    verb syn: to make weak; feeble.
    > The siege of pneumonia *debilitated* her completely.

11. **Impudent** [**im**-pyuh-duhnt]
    adj syn: arrogant; rude; audacious. (***)
    > The teacher raged inwardly at the *impudent* comments of
    > his student, but kept outwardly calm.

13. **Fertilize** [**fur**-ti-ahyz]
    verb syn: to make fertile; to enrich. (*)
    > The newly released product by the company is designed to *fertilize*
    > the farmland.

14. **Denude** [dih-**nood**]
    verb def: to make naked or bare.
    > The storm completely *denuded* the trees.

15. **Dispatch** [dih-**spach**]
    verb def: to send off or away with speed.
    > The spy was *dispatched* to that country.

16. **Presume** [pri-**zoom**]
    verb syn: to take for granted; to assume.
    > Stella *presumes* that her boyfriend must be tired after he drives.

17. **Deliberate** [dih-**lib**-er-it]
    adj syn: carefully considered; studied. (**)
    > Jim's friends try not to talk to him, for he frequently made
    > a *deliberate* lie.

18. **Reverence** [**rev**-er-uhns]

noun syn: awe; veneration; respect. (*)

Many people seemed to pay great *reverence* to the president's comment on the incident that recently occurred.

19. **Eddy** [**ed**-ee]

noun syn: air or wind current.

When water gets pulled down a drain, it forms a small *eddy*.

20. **Grotesque** [groh-**tesk**]

adj def: odd or unnatural in shape

The actors wore dark capes and *grotesque* masks.

21. **Occlude** [uh-**klood**]

verb syn: to shut; to block.

A shadow is thrown across the Earth's surface during a solar eclipse, when the light from the sun is *occluded* by the moon.

22. **Amalgamate** [uh-**mal**-guh-meyt]

verb syn: to mix; to combine. (**)

Giant industries *amalgamated* with Mega Products to form Giant-Mega Products Incorporated.

23. **Immerse** [ih-**murs**]

verb syn: to bathe; to dip; to engross; to preoccupy.

The Japanese snow monkey *immersed* itself in the hot spring.

24. **Girth** [gurth]

noun def: the measure around anything; circumference

The tree Jim found in the forest was about two meters in *girth*.

25. **Linger** [**ling**-ger]

verb def: to remain or stay on in a place longer than is usual. (*)

We *lingered* awhile after the party.

26. **Reluctant** [ri-**luhk**-tuhn]
   adj syn: unwilling; disinclined.
   Andy is *reluctant* to working in a cafeteria.

27. **Facetious** [fuh-**see**-shuhs]
   adj syn: not meant to be taken seriously. (**)
   Justin's *facetious* reply to his teachers made his classmates
   speechless for a moment.

28. **Obsolete** [ob-suh-**leet**]
   adj syn: no longer current; old-fashioned. (*)
   W.H.Auden said that his ideal landscape would include water
   wheels, wooden grain mills, and other forms of *obsolete* machinery.

29. **Quizzical** [**kwiz**-i-kuhl]
   adj syn: odd; queer; comical.
   After Jane heard about the story, she made a *quizzical* expression
   on her face.

30. **Ebullient** [ih-**buhl**-yuhnt]
   adj syn; exhilarated; full of enthusiasm. (**)
   The *ebullient* girl exhausted the baby-sitter, who lacked energy
   to keep up with her.

31. **Gingerly** [**jin**-jer-lee]
   adv def: with great care or cautious; wearily
   Scott *gingerly* opened the cork on the bottle of champagne.

32. **Irascible** [ih-**ras**-uh-buhl]
   adj syn: easily angered.
   Attila the Hun's *irascible* and violent nature made all who
   dealt with him scared.

33. **Bolster** [**bohl**-ster]
   verb syn: to add to; support; uphold.
   They *bolstered* up his claim with new evidence.

34. Renown [ri-**noun**]
adj syn: widespread and high repute.

Dr. Kim is *renown* for the development of ESL education in Korea.

35. Gibberish [**jib**-er-ish]
noun def: meaningless or unintelligent talk or writing

Jenny and Sarah were so excited they could only talk *gibberish*.

36. Reprimand [**rep**-ruh-mand]
verb syn: severe reproof; rebuke. (***)

The teacher immediately *reprimanded* one of his students' misbehavior in class.

37. Apprehend [ap-ri-**hend**]
verb def: to take into custody; to arrest by legal warrant. (*)

The police *apprehended* the burglars.

38. Oblige [uh-**bahyj**]
verb syn: to require; to restrain.

Mr. Weems will *oblige* us with songs.

39. Gratis [**grat**-is]
adj def: without charge or payment; free

The manufacturer provided an extra set of coat buttons *gratis*.

40. Stipulate [**stip**-yuh-leyt]
verb def: to require as an essential condition. (***)

Total disarmament was *stipulated* in the peace treaty.

41. Execute [**ek**-si-kyoot]
verb syn: to carry out; to produce.

The painting was originally *executed* by an unknown artist.

42. Disposal [dih-**spoh**-zuhl]
noun syn: a disposing; allotting of.

She left no will to indicate the *disposal* of her possession.

43. Opulence [op-yuh-luhns]
noun syn: wealth. (**)

Livingston considered his BMW to be a symbol of both *opulence* and style.

44. Gnome [nohm]
noun def: an expert in monetary or financial affair

The reason CBO can't model the 2013 House budget and the Romney-Ryan plan is that they harness markets with competitive bidding. Congress's budget *gnomes* can't handle these dynamic forces.

-Wall Street Journal, August 19, 2012

45. Disclose [dih-sklohz]
verb syn: to cause to appear.

In spring, the violets *disclose* their fragrant petals.

"
The SAT wordbook is very helpful. My reading score was very poor because of the vocabulary words. However, after I studied with this book, I dramatically improved my SAT Critical Reading score. Unlike other books, all the words in this book are easy to memorize. **"**

Jung *(Queen of Peace High School)*

Synonym

1. Furious
- A) Monitor
- B) Extremely angry
- C) Assess
- D) Prescribe
- E) Absolute

2. Apprehensive
- A) Arid
- B) Reservoir
- C) Fearful
- D) Dire
- E) Forecast

3. Meticulous
- A) Severe
- B) Drought
- C) Miserly
- D) Careful
- E) Disquiet

4. Peevish
- A) Irritable
- B) Periphery
- C) Benchmark
- D) Vista
- E) Foliage

5. Impudent

A) Topography
B) Inconsequential
C) Exaggerate
D) Unbroken
E) Shameless

6. Fertilize

A) Reluctant
B) Beget
C) Aggressive
D) Indifferent
E) Solitary

7. Immerse

A) Exhibit
B) Submit
C) Adapt
D) Attribute
E) Bathe

8. Apprehensive

A) Deploy
B) Culminate
C) Fearful
D) Loquacious
E) Incendiary

Answer keys

1) B   2) C   3) D   4) A   5) E   6) B   7) E   8) C

Antonym

1. Amalgamate
   A) Divide
   B) Foresee
   C) Adverse
   D) Domestic
   E) Spurious

2. Reprimand
   A) Disseminate
   B) Extol
   C) Singular
   D) Cursory
   E) Conceal

3. Facetious
   A) Prevalent
   B) Reliable
   C) Dominant
   D) Incentive
   E) Serious

4. Obsolete
   A) Redundant
   B) Versatile
   C) Contemporary
   D) Polished
   E) Rarefied

5. Ebullient
   A) Acerbic
   B) Superfluous
   C) Virulent
   D) Apathetic
   E) Unpalatable

6. Irascible
   A) Multifarious
   B) Nonexistent
   C) Garrulous
   D) Cheerful
   E) Captive

7. Reverence
   A) Promised
   B) Blatant
   C) Mutual
   D) Inclusive
   E) Disrespect

8. Flourish
   A) Cutlery
   B) Cease
   C) Atrophy
   D) Irascible
   E) Augment

9. Inadequate
   A) Sufficient
   B) Aspersion
   C) Undermine
   D) Thwart
   E) Forfeit

Answer keys

1) A 2) B 3) E 4) C 5) D 6) D 7) E 8) B 9) A

1. **Adumbrate** [a-**duhm**-breyt]
   verb syn: to sketch; outline in a shadow way. (**)
   > There was only time to *adumbrate* an escape plan before the cyclone hit.

2. **Disintegrate** [dis-**in**-tuh-greyt]
   verb def: to separate into parts.
   > The old book is gradually *disintegrating* with age.

3. **Distend** [dih-**stend**]
   verb def: to expand by stretching.
   > Habitual overeating had *distended* his stomach.

4. **Deflate** [dee-**fleyt**]
   verb def: to release the air or gas.
   > They *deflated* the tires slightly to allow the truck to drive under the overpass.

5. **Dehydrate** [dee-**hahy**-dreyt]
   verb syn: to lose water or moisture.
   > Milk easily *dehydrates* in the summer.

6. **Aptitude** [**ap**-ti-tood]
   noun syn: capability; ability.
   > She has a unique *aptitude* for mathematics.

7. **Eccentrics** [ik-**sen**-trik]
   adj syn: weird; peculiar. (***)
   > Chris has been known as an *eccentric* teacher among his students.

8. **Erudite** [**er**-yoo-dahyt]
   adj syn: learned; scholarly. (*)
   > The annual meeting of professor brought together the most *erudite*, respected individual in the field.

9. Egocentric [ee-goh-**sen**-trik]

adj def: acting as if things are centered around oneself.

Craig was so *egocentric* that he did not even notice that his comments were hurting Pat's feeling.

10. Altruism [**al**-troo-iz-uhn]

noun def: unselfish concern for other's welfare. (**)

The women's *altruism* revealed itself in the way she gave out money to all who seemed needy.

11. Obsequious [uhb-**see**-kwee-uhs]

noun def: a form of government in which all power is vested in a few persons

The industry is trying to become free of an *oligarchy* of established vendors thus improving services and lowering costs.

12. Oligarchy [**ol**-i-gahr-kee]

noun def: opinion or doctrine at variance with the orthodox

The industry is trying to become free of an *oligarchy* of established vendors thus improving services and lowering costs.

13. Disperse [dih-**spurs**]

verb syn: to break up; to scatter.

The workers *dispersed* after receiving their paychecks, many of them heading for the local bar.

14. Husband [**huhz**-buhnd]

verb syn: to farm; to manage carefully or thriftily. (***)

The farmer's wife *husbanded* the money she had made from her strawberry preserves all year.

15. Stockpile [**stok**-pahyl]

verb syn: to accumulate.

Benjamin always *stockpiles* dried wood for future use.

16. **Extirpate** [ex-ster-peyt]
    verb syn: to pull up; to root up. (**)
    John carefully *extirpated* an unwanted white hair.

17. **Crawl** [krawl]
    verb syn: to move; to progress slowly.
    The line of cars *crawled* behind the slow-moving truck.

18. **Deform** [dih-**fawrm**]
    verb def: to mar the natural form or shape of.
    In the case where the drug was taken during pregnancy, the
    drug's effects *deformed* the infants.

19. **Rescind** [ri-**send**]
    verb syn: to repeal; to cancel. (***)
    The car company *rescinded* the offer of an advertising contract
    it had made to the celebrity after he was accused of murder.

20. **Predicament** [pri-**dik**-muhnt]
    noun def: difficult situation. (*)
    Because he had spent all of his pay, Thomas found himself
    in a miserable *predicament* when his rent bill arrived.

21. **Carnal** [**kahr**-nl]
    adj syn: not spiritual; merely human; temperal. (**)
    Although nothing of a truly intimate, *carnal* nature had occurred
    between the senator and his intern and the senator was forced
    to resign when the scandal broke out.

22. **Deficit** [**def**-uh-sit]
    noun syn: a disadvantage; impairment; handicap.
    The team's major *deficit* is its poor pitching.

23. Pathology [puh-**thol**-uh-jee]
  noun syn: disease, or the study of disease.
      Some people believe that high rates of crime are symptoms of
      an underlying social *pathology*.

24. Conceal [kuhn-**seel**]
  verb syn: to hide; to withdraw.
      He *concealed* the gun under his coat.

25. Disclose [dih-**sklohz**]
  verb syn: to appear, to expose. (**)
      In spring the violets *disclose* their fragrant petals.

26. Haggle [**hag**-uh l]
  verb def: to bargain in a petty, quibbling , and often contentious manner
      They spent hours *haggling* over the price of fish.

27. Stun [stuhn]
  verb syn: to deprive of conscious. (**)
      The blow to his jaw *stunned* him for a moment.

28. Amputate [**am**-pyoo-teyt]
  verb syn: to prune; to lop off; to remove.
      Because of space limitations, the editor *amputated* the last two
      paragraphs of the new report.

29. Limb [lim]
  noun syn: leg; arm; wing.
      The soldier has used an artificial *limb* since he lost one of
      his arms.

30. Underlying [**uhn**-der-lahy-ing]
  adj syn: fundamental; basic. (***)
      There are the *underlying* differences between democracy
      and dictatorship.

31. Imbecility [im-buh-sil-i-tee]
noun def: an instance or point of weakness; feebleness; incapability
Most of the students in the classroom were stunned by the
imbecility of the ideaspresented by this once-respected biologist.

32. Contravene [kon-truh-veen]
verb syn: violate; infringe; transgress. (*)
Franklin never tried to *contravene* any traffic regulations.

33. Probity [proh-bi-tee]
noun syn: honesty; highly-mindedness.
The conscientious witness responded with the utmost *probity* to
all questions posed to her.

34. Disingenuous [dis-in-jen-yoo-uhs]
adj syn: pretending to be candid, simple. (***)
When the Texas billionaire ran for president, many considered his
"jest pain folks" style *disingenuous*.

35. Philander [fi-lan-der]
verb def: to make a love with a woman
He can't seem to stop *philandering*, even now that he's on his
fifth marriage.

36. Presumptuous [pri-zuhmp-choo-uhs]
adj syn: rude; improperly bold. (***)
"I don't want to be *presumptuous,* but why on earth did you
choose red wallpaper?" said Cecil to her hosts.

37. Jocular [jok-yuh-ler]
adj syn: joyful; playful; humorous.
The *jocular* old man entertained his grandchildren with jokes
for hours.

38. Mirth [murth]
noun syn: frivolity; gaiety. (**)
Vera's hilarious jokes contributed to the general *mirth* at the dinner party.

39. Deem [deem]
verb def: to hold an opinion; consider. (*)
Brad *deemed* it wise to refuse the offer.

40. Stagger [**stag**-er]
verb syn: to waver; to begin to doubt.
After *staggering* momentarily, he recognized that he had to make a decision.

41. Paroxysm [**par**-uhk-siz-uhm]
noun syn: any sudden, violent outburst.
After receiving tragic news, he showed an incredible *paroxysm* of rage.

42. Gait [geyt]
noun syn: a manner of walking; stepping.
He taught his horse a specific *gait*.

43. Abreast [uh-**brest**]
adj syn: side by side. (***)
They walked *abreast* down the street.

44. Wreak [reek]
verb syn: to inflict; execute; revenge; avenge. (**)
They *wreaked* havoc on the enemy.

45. Smelt [smelt]
verb def: to melt metal in order to refine it. (*)
We could make jewelry out of this silver ore, but it would look more elegant if we *smelted* it first.

Synonym

1. Mirth
    A) Vital
    B) Gaiety
    C) Trivial
    D) Salient
    E) Undisputed

2. Aptitude
    A) Frugal
    B) Sumptuous
    C) Proficiency
    D) Deposited
    E) Depleted

3. Erudite
    A) Scholastic
    B) Clumped
    C) Displaced
    D) Entrenched
    E) Regained

4. Altruism
    A) Fertilized
    B) Laconic
    C) Voluminous
    D) Verbal
    E) Unselfish

5. Husband

A) Arbitrary
B) Elitist
C) Conserve
D) Virulent
E) Salutary

6. Extirpate

A) Absolute
B) Convoluted
C) Provincial
D) Viable
E) Destroy

7. Rescind

A) Abrogate
B) Multiply
C) Intimidating
D) Interrupt
E) Banning

8. Abreast

A) Forage
B) Ascertain
C) Euphoria
D) Side by side
E) Raunchy

Answer keys

1) B 2) C 3) A 4) E 5) C 6) E 7) A 8) D

Antonym

1. Carnal
- A) Spiritual
- B) Precipitate
- C) Grant
- D) Reapportion
- E) Hasty

2. Conceal
- A) Precarious
- B) Haughty
- C) Reveal
- D) Conciliatory
- E) Dependent

3. Disclose
- A) Impudence
- B) Probity
- C) Largess
- D) Hide
- E) Fidelity

4. Deflate
- A) Adapt
- B) Hasty
- C) Integrate
- D) Glee
- E) Inflate

5. Probity
- A) Monotony
- B) Deceit
- C) Conventionality
- D) Originality
- E) Literacy

6. Presumptuous
    A) Transforming
    B) Polite
    C) Replicating
    D) Displacing
    E) Copying

7. Paroxysm
    A) Calmness
    B) Insult
    C) Vague
    D) Timorous
    E) Effusive

8. Egocentric
    A) Fickle
    B) Recalcitrant
    C) Pugnacious
    D) Spurious
    E) Altruism

9. Predicament
    A) Whimsical
    B) Mock
    C) Solution
    D) Wistful
    E) Moderate

Answer keys

1) A 2) C 3) D 4) E 5) B 6) B 7) A 8) E 9) C

1. **Feign** [feyn]
   verb syn: to make believe; pretend. (**)
   > She is only *feigning*, she isn't really ill.

2. **Irksome** [**urk**-suh m]
   adj def: causing weariness or disgust
   > It is *irksome* that diligence doesn't always guarantee success.

3. **Haunt** [hawnt]
   verb def: to recur persistently to the consciousness.
   > Memories of love continuously *haunted* him.

4. **Mock** [mok]
   verb syn: deceive; challenge; defy; delude. (**)
   > His actions *mocked* people gathering in the convention.

5. **Jibe** [jahyb]
   verb def: to shift from one side to the other
   > Apparently, violent and secretive governments don't *jibe* with their larger mission.

6. **Jingoism** [**jing**-goh-iz-uh m]
   noun def: the spirit; policy, or practice of jingoes; bellicose chauvinism
   > When the war began many people were caught up in a wave of *jingoism*.

7. **Retrospect** [**re**-truth-pokt]
   noun def: in looking back on the past events.
   > It was, in *retrospect*, the happiest day in her life.

8. **Exhort** [ig-**zawart**]
   verb def: to urge or incite by strong appeals. (*)
   > Rob's friends *exhorted* Jeff to beware of ice on the roads when he insisted on driving home in the middle of a snowstorm.

9. **Juggernaut** [**juhg**-er-nawt]
   noun def: any large, overpowering, destructive force or object
   > There was no escaping the *juggernaut* of hype for the studio's biggest summer blockbuster.

10. Stratify [**strat**-uh-fahy]
verb def: to arrange into layers.

Many Indians use the concept of caste to *stratify* society into levels ranging from the "Untouchables" to the Brahmas.

11. Fitful [**fit**-fuhl]
adj syn: intermittent; irregular. (**)

The water came through the tap in *fitful* spurts at first, and they began to pour in a steady flow.

12. Vicarious [vahy-**kair**-ee-uhs]
adj syn: indirect experience. (***)

Great literature broadens our minds by giving us *vicarious* participation in the lives of other people.

13. Insipid [in-**sip**-id]
adj syn: flavorless; uninteresting.

Most TV shows are so *insipid* that you can watch them while reading, without missing a thing.

14. Droll [drohl]
adj def: amusing in a wry, or subtle way, waggish.

Although the play could not be described as hilarious, it was certainly *droll*

15. Ruminate [**roo**-muh-neyt]
verb syn: to contemplate; to reflect upon. (**)

The scholars spent days at the retreat, *ruminating* upon the complexities of the geopolitical situation.

16. Rouse [rouz]
verb def: to bring out of a state of sleep.

He was *roused* to action by courageous words.

17. Soporific [sop-uh-**rif**-ik]
adj syn: sleep or tending to sleep. (**)

The movie proved to be so *soporific* that soon loud snores were heard throughout the theater.

18. **Odious** [oh-dee-uhs]
   adj syn: hateful; contemptible. (**)
   > While most people consider studying vocabulary an *odious* task,
   > there are a few who find it enjoyable.

19. **Discern** [dis-**surn**]
   verb syn: to detect; to notice.
   > I could *discern* the shape of a whale off the starboard bow,
   > but it was too far away to determine its size or species.

20. **Tenacious** [tuh-**ney**-shuhs]
   adj syn: clinging; sticky; persistent. (*)
   > *Tenacious* in pursuit of her goal, she applied for the grant
   > unsuccessfully four times before it was finally approved.

21. **Hilarious** [hi-**lair**-ee-uhs]
   adj syn: arousing great merriment.
   > Michelle enjoyed reading a *hilarious* story.

22. **Onus** [oh-nuh]
   noun def: a difficult or disagreeable obligation
   > The *onus* is on the scientist to prove his hypothesis when
   > observations match the predictions.

23. **Versatile** [**vur**-suh-tl]
   adj syn: adaptable; all-purpose. (**)
   > The *versatile* little gadget can be used to dice vegetables,
   > to open cans, and to whip cream.

24. **Touchy** [tuhch-ee]
   adj def: apt to take offense on sight
   > It always seems a little touchy asking about salaries prior to the nod.

25. Manifest [**man**-uh-fest]

adj syn: obvious.

The fact that she had had plastic surgery was *manifest*, since she looked 20 years younger than she had done the week before.

26. Prospectus [pruh-**spek**-tuhs]

noun def: a document describing the major feature.

Don't buy the new stock offering until you read the *prospectus* carefully.

27. Protean [**pro**-tee-uhn]

adj def: readily assuming different form or characters. (*)

The *protean* Scarlet Pimpernel could play a wide variety of different characters convincingly.

28. Arbitrate [**ahr**-bi-treyt]

verb syn: mediate; negotiate. (**)

Since the couple could not come to agreement, a judge was forced to *arbitrate* their divorce proceedings.

29. Articulate [ahr-**tik**-yuh-lit]

adj def: well-spoken; to express oneself clearly.

She is such an *articulate* defender of labor that unions are among her strongest supporters.

30. Arbitrary [**ahr**-bi-ter-ee]

adj def: depending solely on individual will.

Nancy won a prize, but not Fred, making the judges' decisions seem completely *arbitrary*.

31. Mandate [man-**deyt**]

noun syn: accreditation; authorization.

The new policy on gays in the military went into effect as soon as the president issued his *mandate* about it.

32. Vulgar [**vuhl**-ger]
adj syn: indecent; obscene; lewd. (***)
> His *vulgar* behavior destroyed his reputation he had built up for the past 25 years.

33. Consortium [kuhn-**sawr**-shee-uhn]
noun def: a combination of financial institutions.
> In a wrongful death action, the surviving spouse commonly seeks damages for loss of *consortium*.

34. Irrevocable [ih-**rev**-uh-kuh-buhl]
adj syn: conclusive; irreversible. (**)
> Once he had pushed the red button, the president's decision to launch missile was *irrevocable*.

35. Serendipity [ser-uhn-**dip**-i-ty]
noun def: habit of making fortunate discoveries by chance. (***)
> Rosemary's *serendipity* revealed itself in many ways, such as in her habit of finding money on the street.

36. Ominous [**om**-uh-nuhs]
adj syn: menacing; threatening; indicating misfortune. (**)
> The sky was filled with *ominous* dark clouds before the storm.

37. Enact [en-**akt**]
verb def: to make into an act.
> Congress has *enacted* a new tax law.

38. Maritime [**mar**-i-tahym]
adj def: connected with the sea in relation to navigation.
> At the *maritime* museum, historic ships and sailing equipment are displayed.

39. Junket [**juhng**-kit]
noun def: a pleasure excursion, as a picnic or outing
> The senator has been criticized for expensive *junkets* to foreign countries.

40. Sanitize [san-i-tahyz]
verb def: to make less offensive.

He *sanitized* a document before releasing it to the press.

41. Reputation [rep-yuh-**tey**-shuhn]
noun def: publicly recognized name or standing.

Mr. Hennessey has spent whole his life building up a *reputation* as a capable lawyer.

42. Tendency [**ten**-duhn-see]
noun syn: inclination; bent.

Steve has a strong *tendency* to talk too much.

43. Lechery [**lech**-uh-ree]
noun def: unrestrained or excessive indulgence of sexual desire

The climate of lunacy and *lechery* is not insalubrious for him.

44. Detrimental [de-truh-**men**-tl]
adj syn: harmful; negative. (**)

It is generally acknowledged that cigarette smoking can be *detrimental* to people's health.

45. Deter [dih-**tur**]
verb syn: to prevent; stop; hinder. (***)

Some sociologists claim that the death penalty does not really *deter* criminals from committing crimes.

Synonym

1. Mock
- A) Cogent
- B) Derive
- C) Necessary
- D) Protocol
- E) Emit

2. Exhort
- A) Resist
- B) Surpass
- C) Abase
- D) Encourage
- E) Reject

3. Mandate
- A) Cogent
- B) Derive
- C) Mixed
- D) Protocol
- E) Emit

4. Vicarious
- A) Indirect
- B) Harmless
- C) Liberator
- D) Indigenous
- E) Benign

5. Ruminate
    A) Riddle
    B) Cryptic
    C) Exam
    D) Insect
    E) Reptile

6. Soporific
    A) Axiom
    B) Sleepy
    C) Geometric
    D) Sinister
    E) Circumlocution

7. Discern
    A) Sterile
    B) Disguise
    C) Strength
    D) Modest
    E) Recognize

8. Detrimental
    A) Copious
    B) Impeccable
    C) Venerable
    D) Harmful
    E) Delegation

Answer keys

1) B 2) D 3) C 4) A 5) C 6) B 7) E 8) D

Antonym

1. Vulgar
   A) Decent
   B) Clumsy
   C) Despot
   D) Troupe
   E) Gourmand

2. Rectitude
   A) Assuage
   B) Urbanity
   C) Dishonesty
   D) Endure
   E) Discomfort

3. Protean
   A) Swindler
   B) Anarchist
   C) Serenity
   D) Unchangeable
   E) Convention

4. Articulate
   A) Novice
   B) Validation
   C) Coward
   D) Tenacity
   E) Unclear

5. Vulgar
   A) Decent
   B) Comet
   C) Solid
   D) Canter
   E) Molt

6. Irrevocable
    A) Unmarred
    B) Blemish
    C) Alterable
    D) Arresting
    E) Vicious

7. Ominous
    A) Vogue
    B) Auspicious
    C) Arid
    D) Boisterous
    E) Fearless

8. Deter
    A) Coerced
    B) Supple
    C) Magnanimous
    D) Persuade
    E) Somber

9. Manifest
    A) Ambiguous
    B) Convene
    C) Tribulation
    D) Vivacious
    E) Epidemic

Answer keys

1) A 2) C 3) D 4) E 5) A 6) C 7) B 8) D 9) A

1. Levee [lev-ee]
noun def: an embankment designed to prevent the flooding of a river
They built a *levee* to protect the city; however, the water rose to thirty feet and destroyed everything they had built in their town.

2. Limn [lim]
verb def: to represent in drawing or painting
He *limned* the scene in the courtroom so perfectly that I could practically see it.

3. Nebulous [neb-yuh-luhs]
adj syn: hazy; vague; indistinct. (***)
The candidate's *nebulous* plans to fight crime lacked the concrete detail that skeptical voters demanded.

4. Nefarious [ni-fair-ee-uhs]
adj syn: very wicked.
The villain's crimes, though various, were one and all *nefarious*.

5. Appeal [uh-peel]
verb syn: to ask for aid; support; mercy; sympathy.
The college *appealed* to its alumni for funds.

6. Refute [ri-fyoot]
verb syn: to disprove; rebut. (***)
The defense called several respectable witnesses who were able to *refute* the false testimony of the prosecution's sole witness.

7. Lurid [loo-r-id]
adj syn: harsh; shocking; sensational; glowing.
The policeman nearly had a heart attack when he saw the *lurid* headlines about his past indiscretion.

8. Chasten [chen-suhn]
verb syn: to restrain; to subdue; to punish. (**)
Age has *chastened* his violent temper.

9. **Itinerant** [ahy-**tin**-er-uhnt]
   adj def: wondering from place to place. syn: unsettled.
   The *itinerant* tomcat came by the Johansson homestead every six months or so.

10. **Litany** [**lit**-n-ee]
    noun def: a ceremonial or liturgical form of prayer
    We heard the whole *litany* of their complaints.

11. **Subdued** [suhb-**dood**]
    adj syn: less intense; quieter. (**)
    In the hospital, visitors spoke in a *subdued* tone of voice for fear of disturbing the patients.

12. **Mangy** [**meyn**-jee]
    adj def: contemptible; mean; a mangy trick
    There was a *mangy* car covered in rust.

13. **Contentious** [kuhn-**ten**-shhs]
    adj syn: quarrelsome; disagreeable; belligerent. (**)
    The *contentious* gentleman in the bar angrily ridiculed whatever anyone said.

14. **Sanguine** [**sang**-gwin]
    adj syn: ruddy; cheerfully optimistic. (**)
    A *sanguine* person thinks the glass is half full, while a depressed person thinks it is half empty.

15. **Natal** [**neyt**-l]
    adj def: relating to birth.
    The pregnant woman and her husband searched for a hospital specializing in *natal* care.

16. Mutability [myoo-tuh-**bi**-luh-ti]

noun syn: changeability. (**)

> We need stable substances for this solution, and the *mutability* of
> this compound makes it unsuitable for our experiment.

17. Manumit [mah-yuh-**mit**]

verb def: to release from slavery or servitude

> Although he was an outspoken defender of liberty, Anderson did
> not *manumit* his own slaves until he was on his deathbed.

18. Derivative [dih-**riv**-uh-tiv]

adj syn: copied; adapted; not original.

> The TV show was so obviously *derivative* of Seinfeld that
> viewers who prize originality were not interested in watching it.

19. Gauche [gohsh]

adj syn: lacking social grace; sensitivity. (***)

> Their exquisite manners always make me feel *gauche*.

20. Sublime [suh-**blahym**]

adj def: elevated or lofty in thought.

> Paradise Lost is *sublime* poetry.

21. Nubile [noo-**bahul**]

adj def: suitable for marriage, especially in regard to age

> Evolution, in short, favors *nubile* females who still look as though
> they have a great many years of fertility ahead of them.

22. Erudite [er-yoo-**dahyt**]

adj syn: learned; scholarly. (**)

> The annual meeting of professors brought together the most
> *erudite*, respected individuals in the field.

23. Lout [lout]

noun def: an awkward, stupid person; clumsy

> Howard's rude behavior at the country club earned him a
> reputation as a *lout*.

24. Cognate [kog-neyt]
adj def: mental process by which knowledge is acquired. (*)
The young man was *cognate* to several royal families, making him a prospect on the marriage market.

25. Monastic [muh-nas-tik]
adj def: extremely plain or secluded.
The philosopher retired to his *monastic* lodgings to contemplate life free from any worldly distraction.

26. Correlation [kawr-uh-ley-shuhn]
noun syn: association; mutual relationship.
All too often, there is little *correlation* between the amount of money someone makes and her intelligence.

27. Corroborate [kuh-rob-uh-reyt]
verb syn: to confirm; to verify. (**)
Fingerprints *corroborated* the witness's testimony that he saw the defendant in the victim's apartment.

28. Corrugated [kawr-uh-gey-tud]
verb def: to mold in a shape with parallel grooves and ridges.
The *corrugated* tin roofs of the shantytown glinted in the haze.

29. Fluctuate [fluhk-choo-yet]
verb syn: to alternate; waver. (**)
Certain stock prices *fluctuated* so much that it was risky to invest in them.

30. Impassive [im-pas-iv]
adj syn: without feeling; impenetrable; stoical. (*)
Refusing to let the enemy see how deeply shaken he was by his capture, the prisoners kept his face *impassive*.

31. Virulent [vir-yuh-luhnt]
adj syn: extremely poisonous; hostile. (***)
While playing with his friends in the field, Tom got a lot of *virulent* bites from many different kinds of mosquitoes.

32. Orgy [awr-jee]
noun def: wild, drunken or licentious festivity or revelry

Joshua found a national *orgy* of thrill seeking and risk taking.

33. Hone [hohn]
verb syn: to sharpen; put a point on. (***)

Esther spent numerous hours studying in the library to *hone* her test skills and strategies.

34. Divination [div-uh-**ney**-shuhn]
noun def: the art of predicting future. (**)

In Ancient Greece, people wanting to know their fate would visit the priests at Delphi, who were supposedly skilled at *divination*.

35. Concede [kuhn-**seed**]
verb syn: to yield; admit.

Ralph *conceded* that he should have checked that he had enough gas before driving into the wilderness.

36. Opiate [**oh**-pee-it]
noun def: a drug containing opium or its derivatives

Opiate pain relievers, such as morphine or fentanyl, may be needed to control severe pain.

37. Paradigm [**par**-uh-dahym]
noun syn: model; example; pattern.

Pavlov's experiment in which he trains a dog to salivate on hearing a bell is a *paradigm* of the conditioned-response experiment in behavioral psychology.

38. Pertinent [**pur**-tn-uhnt]
adj syn: applicable; appropriate. (*)

The supervisor felt that his employee's complaints were *pertinent* and mentioned them in the meeting.

39. Pernicious [per-**nish**-uhs]
adj syn: very destructive; harmful. (**)
> The Athenians argued that Socrates' teaching had a *pernicious* effect on young and susceptible minds; therefore, they condemned him.

40. Perpetuate [per-**pech**-oo-yet]
verb syn: to make something last; preserve. (**)
> Some critics attacked The Adventure of Huckleberry Finn because they believe Twain's book *perpetuates* a false image of African-Americans in this country.

41. Vague [veyg]
adj syn: not clear; opaque.
> A *vague* shape in the dark shocked her.

42. Winsome [**win**-suhm]
adj syn: charming; happily engaging. (***)
> Dawn gave the customs officers a *winsome* smile, and they let her pass without searching her bags.

43. Macabre [muh-**kah**-bruh]
adj def: gruesome and horrifying; ghastly
> Police discovered a *macabre* scene inside the house.

44. Germane [jer-**meyn**]
adj syn: pertinent. (**)
> The judge would not allow the testimony to be heard by the jury because it was not *germane* to the case.

45. Sophistry [**sof**-uh-stree]
noun syn: deceptive; reasoning; argumentation.
> The politicians used *sophistry* to cloud the issue whenever he was asked a tough question in a debate.

Synonym

1. Versatile
    A) Reckoning
    B) Multi-talented
    C) Truce
    D) Adjournment
    E) Perennial

2. Nebulous
    A) Opaque
    B) Morbid
    C) Cloister
    D) Convent
    E) Parole

3. Lurid
    A) Quarantine
    B) Pupil
    C) Gruesome
    D) Glut
    E) Enliven

4. Chasten
    A) Boast
    B) Flatter
    C) Modest
    D) Innate
    E) Restrain

5. Subdued
A) Void
B) Sequester
C) Evade
D) Quiet
E) Fickle

6. Sanguine
A) Inconsistency
B) Cheerful
C) Placid
D) Fecundity
E) Deviation

7. Gauche
A) Tactless
B) Appealing
C) Miserable
D) Delineation
E) Tactile

8. Nefarious
A) Tame
B) Adroit
C) Wicked
D) Sedition
E) Insurrection

Answer keys

1) B 2) A 3) C 4) E 5) D 6) B 7) A 8) C

Antonym

1. Detached
- A) Intermission
- B) Dismay
- C) Attach
- D) Distort
- E) Disband

2. Perplex
- A) Clarify
- B) Congest
- C) Grateful
- D) Hardy
- E) Euphoria

3. Corroborate
- A) Revolt
- B) Deny
- C) Impeach
- D) Fictitious
- E) Offspring

4. Virulent
- A) Futile
- B) Chaos
- C) Episodic
- D) Cynic
- E) Gentle

5. Conjecture
- A) Abdicate
- B) Revolt
- C) Throne
- D) Resign
- E) Proven

6. Pernicious
    A) Martyr
    B) Xenophobia
    C) Innocuous
    D) Derelict
    E) Optimist

7. Dauntless
    A) Daunt
    B) Concrete
    C) Futile
    D) Fertile
    E) Apothecary

8. Germane
    A) Delude
    B) Contentious
    C) Impertinent
    D) Brook
    E) Implement

9. Contrite
    A) Cease
    B) Impenitent
    C) Realm
    D) Concur
    E) Patrimony

Answer keys

1) C 2) A 3) B 4) E 5) E 6) C 7) A 8) C 9) B

1. Solicit [suh-**lis**-it]

verb syn: to request honestly; to seek. (**)

Knowing she needed to have a solid majority for the budget to pass, the mayor telephoned all the members of city council to *solicit* their votes.

2. Contrite [kuhn-**trahyt**]

adj def: sorry for past misdeed. syn: to regret. (***)

The public is often willing to forgive celebrities who are involved in some scandal, as long as they appear *contrite*.

3. Painstaking [**peynz**-teng-king]

adj def: showing hard working.

The new high-frequency word list is the result of *painstaking* efforts on the part of our research staff.

4. Stoic [**stoh**-ik]

adj def: indifferent to or unaffected by emotion.

While most of the mourners wept, the dead woman's husband kept up a *stoic*, unemotional facade.

5. Precocious [pri-**koh**-shuhs]

adj def: mature at an unusually early age.

Picasso was so *precocious* as an artist that, at nine, he is said to have painted better pictures than his teacher had painted.

6. Obsequious [uhb-**see**-kwee-uhs]

adj syn: slavishly attentive; fawning; toady; flatter. (***)

Why are some waiters in fancy restaurants so *obsequious*?

7. Insular [**in**-suh-ler]

adj syn: isolated; detached.

The inhabitants of the *insular* little village were shocked when Mrs. Malone set up a belly-dancing school in her home.

8. Insinuate [in-**sin**-yoo-yet]

verb syn: to imply; hint. (*)

When you said I looked robust, were you trying to *insinuate* I am getting fat?

9. **Cynic** [**sin**-ik]
   noun def: one who is skeptical or distrustful of human motives.
   > A born *cynic*, Sydney was suspicious whenever anyone gave her a gift "with no strings attached."

10. **Ascendancy** [uh-**sen**-dahn-see]
    noun def: state of rising; ascending power or control.
    > The devious politician's *ascendancy* to the top ranks of government seemed inevitable.

11. **Disconcerting** [dis-kuhn-**surt**]
    adj syn: bewildering; perplexing; slightly disturbing. (**)
    > Brad found his mother-in-law's hostile manner so *disconcerting* that he acted like a fool in her presence.

12. **Discordant** [dis-**kawr**-dnt]
    adj syn: harsh-sounding; badly out of tune.
    > The harpsichord sounded completely *discordant* after not having been played for 50 years.

13. **Impoverish** [im-**pov**-er-ish]
    verb syn: to reduce to poverty. (*)
    > Bad farming practices *impoverished* the soil.

14. **Pomp** [pomp]
    noun syn: ostentatious; splendid display.
    > The official was accompanied by all the *pomps* of his high position.

15. **Dissent** [dih-**sent**]
    verb syn: to disagree; to differ in. (**)
    > Two of the justices *dissented* from the majority decision.

16. **Revere** [ri-**veer**]
    verb syn: to respect; to venerate.
    > The child *revered* her mother.

17. **Overlook** [oh-ver-**look**]
    verb syn: to fail to perceive; notice; consider. (***)
    He accidentally *overlooked* many misspelled words.

18. **Incarcerate** [in-**kahr**-suh-reyt]
    verb def: to put in jail. syn: to confine.
    The thief had been *incarcerated* for two years, but he got out
    on parole after six months.

19. **Persevere** [pur-suh-**veer**]
    verb def: to continue despite difficulties. (*)
    Although several of her teammates dropped out of the marathon,
    Laura *persevered*.

20. **Champion** [**cham**-pee-uhn]
    verb syn: to defend; support. (***)
    Ursula continued to *champion* the rights of the prisoner, even after
    it was proven beyond a doubt that he was guilty.

21. **Charlatan** [**shahr**-luh-tn]
    noun syn: quack; fake. (**)
    "That *charlatan* prescribed the wrong medicine for me!"
    complained the patient.

22. **Chary** [**chair**-ee]
    adj syn: watchful; cautious.
    Mindful of the fate of the Titanic, the captain was *chary*
    of navigating the iceberg-filled sea.

23. **Assuage** [uh-**sweyj**]
    verb syn: to make milder; less severe. (*)
    Taking aspirin *assuages* one's pain.

24. **Peerless** [**peer**-lis]
    adj def: having no equal; matchless; unrivaled
    The show's enduring success was a testimony to the *peerless* talents
    of its ensemble cast.

25. Petulance [pech-uh-luhns]
noun syn: rudeness; peevishness.
> The child's *petulance* annoyed the teacher, who liked her young students to be cheerful and cooperative.

26. Variegate [vair-ee-i-geyt]
verb syn: to give variety to; diversity. (**)
> The *variegated* foliage of the jungle allows it to support thousands of different animal species.

27. Exasperate [ig-zas-puh-reyt]
verb syn: to irritate; to annoy. (****)
> Sharon was *exasperated* by the yelling of her neighbor's children, since she was trying to study.

28. Exculpate [ek-skuhl-peyt]
verb def: to free from blame. (*)
> When someone else confessed to the crime, the previous suspect was *exculpated*.

29. Peccadillo [pek-uh-dil-oh]
noun def: a very minor or slight sin or offense
> "The only interest, as far as I can see, is that the CIA is barred from domestic surveillance, and that they're destroying files. Who knows how many and which. But by today's standards of government malpractice, it's a minor *peccadillo*."
> -Judy Leecraft

30. Rebuttal [ri-buht-l]
noun syn: refutation. def: response with contrary evidence. (***)
> The defense lawyer confidently listened to the prosecutor sum up his case, making sure that she could answer his arrangement in her *rebuttal*.

31. Headstrong [hed-strawng]
adj syn: willful; stubborn.
> Bill was considered as a *headstrong* student when he was in high school.

32. Complacent [kuhm-**ple**-suhnt]
adj syn: self-satisfied; smug. (***)
> Phillip smiled *complacently* as he was showered with compliments for his handling of the Buckman deal.

33. Truculent [**truhk**-yuh-luhnt]
adj syn: aggressive; hostile. (**)
> Hitler's *truculent* behavior in demanding more territory for Germany made it clear that was inevitable.

34. Truncate [**truhng**-keyt]
verb syn: to cut off; to shorten; replace. (**)
> The manuscript of the play appeared *truncated*; the last page ended in the middle of a scene, halfway through the first act.

35. Debilitate [dih-**bil**-i-teyt]
verb syn: to make weak; feeble.
> The siege of pneumonia *debilitated* her completely.

36. Expedient [ik-**spee**-dee-uhnt]
adj syn: convenient; efficient; practical.
> It was considered more *expedient* to send the fruit directly to the retailer instead of through a middleman.

37. Expatriate [eks-**pey**-tree-yet]
verb def: to drive someone from his/her own country.
> Imelda Marcos was *expatriated* from the Philippines after her husband deposed.

38. Tableau [ta-**bloh**]
noun syn: vivid description; striking scene. (*)
> The tourists admired the famous painter's lifelike *tableau* of the Last Supper.

39. Tacit [**tas**-it]
adj syn: silently understood; implied. (**)
> Although not a word had been said, everyone in the room knew that a *tacit* agreement had been made about which course of action to take.

40. Preempt [pree-empt]

verb def: to acquire or appropriate before someone else.

A political issue *preempted* by the opposition party.

41. Demure [dih-myoor]

adj syn: modest; shy.

The *demure* heroines of Victorian fiction have given way to today's stronger, more opinionated, and more independent female characters.

42. Denigrate [den-i-grate]

verb syn: to criticize; belittle. (**)

The firm's new president tried to explain his plans for improving the company without seeming to *denigrate* the work of his predecessors.

43. Subterfuge [suhb-ter-fyooj]

noun def: trick or tactic used to avoid something. (***)

Spies who are not skilled in the art of *subterfuge* are generally exposed before too long.

44. Stalwart [stawl-wert]

adj syn: sturdy; robust. (**)

They counted on the party *stalwarts* for support in the off-year campaign.

45. Cliche [klee-shey]

noun syn: trite; hackneyed; stereotype.

Dr. Smith made a speech filled with *cliché* about how to prepare for the SATs.

Synonym

1. Stalwart
- A) Valiant
- B) Coagulate
- C) Incredible
- D) Culprit
- E) Concur

2. Demure
- A) Facility
- B) Fallacious
- C) Reserved
- D) Profuse
- E) Congenial

3. Debilitate
- A) Decade
- B) Diurnal
- C) Doctrine
- D) Weaken
- E) Condolence

4. Tacit
- A) Discredit
- B) Culpable
- C) Cease
- D) Homicide
- E) Not talkative

5. Truncate
    A) Cut off
    B) Affluent
    C) Decimal
    D) Fracture
    E) Heterogeneous

6. Truculent
    A) Memento
    B) Hostile
    C) Enhance
    D) Mollify
    E) Eligible

7. Exasperate
    A) Alliteration
    B) Macrobiotics
    C) Eject
    D) Provoke
    E) Intercede

8. Exasperate
    A) Stint
    B) Plague
    C) Annoy
    D) Sedulous
    E) Vindictive

Answer keys

1) A 2) C 3) D 4) E 5) A 6) B 7) D 8) C

Antonym

1. Petulance
- A) Ablution
- B) Lexicon
- C) Pleasant
- D) Liaison
- E) Hasty

2. Assuage
- A) Morbid
- B) Natal
- C) Cognate
- D) Novelty
- E) Exacerbate

3, Champion
- A) Support
- B) Oppose
- C) Pyre
- D) Quintessence
- E) Radiate

4. Incarcerate
- A) Free from
- B) Regent
- C) Preclude
- D) Phobia
- E) Paternal

5. Revere
- A) Exponent
- B) Despise
- C) Rapport
- D) Interregnum
- E) Primal

6. Impoverish
 A) Poverty
 B) Umbrage
 C) Rich
 D) Valor
 E) Tremor

7. Insinuate
 A) Withhold
 B) Perturbation
 C) Tacit
 D) Prosper
 E) Scribe

8. Exculpate
 A) Allege
 B) Infectious
 C) Patronage
 D) Incriminate
 E) Abstruse

9. Rebuttal
 A) Versatile
 B) Proof
 C) Indict
 D) Somber
 E) Fidgety

Answer keys

1) C 2) E 3) B 4) A 5) B 6) C 7) A 8) D 9) B

1. **Cavalier** [Kav-uh-**leer**]
   adj syn: carefree; happy.
   > The nobleman's *cavalier* attitude toward the suffering of
   > the peasants working for him made them hate him.

2. **Skeptical** [**skep**-ti-kuhl]
   adj syn: doubting.
   > I am *skeptical* about the new health plan; I want some proof that
   > it can work for me.

3. **Requite** [ri-**kwahyt**]
   verb syn: to return; pay. (**)
   > Thanks for offering to lend me $500,000, but I know I will never
   > be able to *requite* your generosity.

4. **Beget** [bih-**get**]
   verb def: to cause or produce an effect
   > Bruce passed away three days ago without *begetting* a
   > legitimate son.

5. **Portent** [**pawr**-tent]
   noun syn: omen.
   > Kylie quacked in fear as she watched a black cat cross her path,
   > a *portent* of bad luck in the future.

6. **Tryst** [trahyst]
   noun def: agreement between lovers to meet; rendezvous.
   > The knight arranged a secret *tryst* with the nobleman's wife deep
   > in the forest.

7. **Expropriate** [eks-**proh**-pree-yet]
   verb def: to seize ownership of. (**)
   > When the communists came to power in China, they
   > *expropriated* most businesses and turned them over to
   > government-appointed managers.

8. **Bilk** [bilk]

   verb syn: to cheat; fraud. (**)

   Though the lawyer seemed honest, the woman feared he would try
   to *bilk* her out of her money.

9. **Blanch** [blahnch]

   verb def: pale; take the color out of.

   The murderess *blanched* when the man she thought she had killed
   walked into the club.

10. **Pious** [**pahy**-uhs]

    adj syn: devout.

    The challenge for church people today is how to be *pious* in
    the best sense, that is, to be devout without becoming hypocritical
    or sanctimonious.

11. **Terse** [turs]

    adj syn: concise; brief. (**)

    Jennifer's *terse* style of writing was widely praised for coming
    directly to the point.

12. **Iconoclast** [ahy-**koh**-uh-klast]

    noun def: one who attacks traditional beliefs. (**)

    His lack of regard for traditional beliefs soon established him as
    an *iconoclast*.

13. **Depravity** [dih-**prav**-i-ty]

    noun syn: corruption; wickedness. (*)

    Even Roman who had grown accustomed to perversions and
    immorality during Tiberius's reign were shocked by the
    depravity of the emperor Caligula.

14. **Aloof** [uh-**loof**]

    adverb syn: detached; indifference. (*)

    The newcomer remained *aloof* from all our activities and therefore
    made no new friends.

15. **Ambivalence** [am-**biv**-uh-luhns]
noun def: having two or more feelings or attitudes.
> Angela was *ambivalent* toward her impending marriage; at times she was eager to go ahead, while at other times she wanted to call it off.

16. **Calumny** [**kal**-uhm-nee]
noun def: false and malicious accusation. (**)
> The unscrupulous politicians used *calumny* to bring down his opponent in the senatorial race.

17. **Ingrate** [in-**greyt**]
noun syn: ungrateful person. (*)
> That *ingrate,* Bob sneered at the tie I gave him.

18. **Invigorate** [in-**vig**-uh-reyt]
verb syn: to give energy to; to stimulate. (**)
> As her car climbed the mountain road, Lucinda felt *invigorated* by the clear air and the cool breezes.

19. **Exculpate** [ek-**skuhl**-peyt]
verb syn: to clear of blame or fault; vindicate.
> The adversarial legal system is intended to convict those who are guilty and *exculpate* those who are innocent.

20. **Enervate** [**en**-er-veyt]
verb def: to reduce the energy or strength. (****)
> ant: to energize; strengthen.
> The stress of the operation left her feeling *enervated* for about two weeks.

21. **Drudgery** [**druhy**-uh-ree]
noun def: menial, distasteful, dull, or hard work
> "It is quite true and quite proper that better eating habits, better care and less *drudgery* have made American women look ten years younger than their mothers did at the same age."
> -Marya Mannes

22. Candor [kan-der]
   noun syn: honesty of expression. (**)
   > The *candor* of his confession impressed his parents, and they gave him a light punishment as a result.

23. Dissuade [dih-**sweyd**]
   verb def: to deter by advice or punishment.
   > She *dissuaded* him from leaving home.

24. Animosity [an-uh-**mos**-i-tees]
   noun def: a feeling of strong dislike.
   > We found a deeply seated *animosity* between the sisters.

25. Craven [**krey**-vuhn]
   adj syn: cowardly. (**)
   > The *craven* lion cringed in the corner of his cage, terrified of the mouse.

26. Frivolity [fri-**vol**-i-tees]
   noun def: the quality or state of being frivolous. (*)
   > He had a hard time living down the *frivolity*.

27. Ratify [**rat**-uh-fahy]
   verb def: to confirm by expressing consent.
   > The senate *ratified* a constitutional amendment.

28. Ensconce [en-**skons**]
   verb def: to settle securely or smugly
   > I found Jin in the library, *ensconced* in an armchair.

29. Supplant [suh-**plant**]
   verb syn: to replace; to displace. (**)
   > Did the other woman actually *supplant* Princess Diana in Prince's Charles affectations or did Charles never love Diana at all?

30. Pilfer [**pil**-fer]
verb syn: to steal. (***)
> Marianne did not *pilfer* the money for herself but rather for her
> sick brother, who needed medicine.

31. Atrophy [a-**truh**-fee]
verb syn: to waste away.
> After three months in a cast, Stan's biceps had *atrophied*
> somewhat; however, he was sure that if he pumped iron
> for a while he would soon build them up.

32. Irascible [ih-**ras**-ci-buhl]
adj syn: easily angered. (**)
> Attila the Hun's *irascible* and violent nature made all who
> dealt with him fear for their lives.

33. Eloquence [**el**-uh-kwuhns]
noun def: expressiveness or persuasive speech.
> The crowds were stirred by Martin Luther King's *eloquence*.

34. Savory [**sey**-vuh-ree]
adj syn: pleasure; agreeable in taste. (*)
> The banquet guests consumed the *savory* treats with pleasure.

35. Idiosyncrasy [id-ee-uh-**sing**-kruh-see]
noun def: individual trait, usually odd in nature. (***)
> One of Richard Nixon's little *idiosyncrasies* was his liking for
> ketchup on cottage cheese.

36. Impediment [im-**ped**-uh-muhnt]
noun syn: barrier; obstacle.
> Ludmila's speech *impediment* made it difficult to understand what
> he was saying.

37. Impetus [im-pi-tuhs]
noun syn: a moving force.

The grant for building the opera house gave *impetus* to the city's culture life.

38. Fickle [fik-uhl]
adj syn: likely to change; caprice; whimsical. (**)

Mike got tired of the *fickle* weather in NYC.

39. Recalcitrant [ri-kal-si-truhnt]
adj syn: not obedient; refractory. (**)

The police chief was extremely good at dealing with *recalcitrant* police officers.

40. Pugnacious [puhg-ney-shuhs]
adj syn: quarrelsome; ready to fight.

The serene eighty-year-old used to be a *pugnacious* troublemaker in her youth, but she is softer now.

41. Lucrative [loo-kruh-tiv]
adj syn: profitable; moneymaking.

Tim established his own *lucrative* business when he was a high school student.

42. Spurious [spyoor-ee-uhs]
adj syn: false; counterfeit. (***)

Unaccustomed to the design of the new hundred-dollar bills, many storekeepers rejected them as *spurious*.

43. Savant [sa-vahnt]
noun def: learned person.

The *savant* was happy to give advice to those who were not as intellectually gifted as she was.

44. Pungent [**puhn**-juhnt]

adj syn: stinging. def: sharp in taste or smell. (***)

> The *pungent* odor of ripe Limburger cheese appealed to Simone but made Stanley gag.

45. Abhor [ab-**hawr**]

verb syn: to loath; detest; hate. (**)

> After she repeatedly failed to learn the Pythagorean theorem, Susan began to *abhor* geometry.

" Mastering Core SAT Words *by William H. Shin is a condensed book of the common vocabulary that appears on the SAT exam. Its daily list of vocabulary words gives students an organized way of learning and studying for the Critical Reading section of the SAT. In addition to its systematic teaching techniques, the book contains a drill after every section to ensure the student's complete understanding of these words. The specific words that William H. Shin compiled in this book will improve the student's comprehension in not only the sentence completions, but also the reading comprehension.* **"**

Sujin Prudence Cho *(Bergen County Academies)*
Admitted to Rutgers, Pharmacy

❝ *Taking the SAT is a critical step for an individual seeking to pursue his or her career at a college. William Shin's book,* Mastering Core SAT Words, *is an excellent source for gaining support when memorizing vocabulary words that are commonly present on the SAT. This book contains 1,395 SAT vocabulary words, more than enough to increase an individual's Critical Reading score. As a former student of Mr. Shin, I am more than happy to recommend this book to people worldwide. He helped me enhance my SAT Critical Reading and Writing scores in a short amount of time. His support, through his experience and knowledge, as well as unique studying routines, affected me greatly and positively. Because practice is a key factor in obtaining a high score on the SAT, Mr. Shin provided me with numerous practice tests and questions similar to those in this book. The results were evident from my SAT scores, which were high enough to make both Mr. Shin and myself proud. With instructor Shin's help, I have received numerous acceptance letters from colleges that I had applied to, including Rutgers University.* **❞**

Esther Kang *(Ridgefield Memorial High School)*
Admitted to the Ernest Mario School of Pharmacy at Rutgers University

Synonym

1. Pungent
    A) Contravene
    B) Piquant
    C) Terminal
    D) Extort
    E) Resurgent

2. Lucrative
    A) Sophistry
    B) Insomnia
    C) Profitable
    D) Disrupt
    E) Ascribe

3. Fickle
    A) Caprice
    B) Transgress
    C) Turbulent
    D) Prosperous
    E) Sedate

4. Eloquence
    A) Pyromania
    B) Potential
    C) Compel
    D) Fluent
    E) Novelty

5. Atrophy
>A) Disappear
>B) Nomenclature
>C) Obnoxious
>D) Enumerate
>E) Paternal

6. Craven
>A) Matron
>B) Magnify
>C) Coward
>D) Mediate
>E) Levitate

7. Exculpate
>A) Eject
>B) Holocaust
>C) Abjure
>D) Literate
>E) Free from blame

8. Skeptical
>A) Speculative
>B) Sarcastic
>C) Profound
>D) Reprehensible
>E) Raconteur

Answer keys

1) B 2) C 3) A 4) D 5) A 6) C 7) E 8) B

Antonym

1. Abhor
    A) Disaffected
    B) Seduce
    C) Entice
    D) Infallible
    E) Adore

2. Spurious
    A) Genuine
    B) Eulogy
    C) Exacerbate
    D) Elicit
    E) Interdict

3. Recalcitrant
    A) Controversy
    B) Culprit
    C) Egocentric
    D) Obey
    E) Decimal

4. Impediment
    A) Viaduct
    B) Embellish
    C) Congenital
    D) Aid
    E) Diffract

5. Irascible
    A) Quotidian
    B) Calm
    C) Abdicate
    D) Affluent
    E) Viaduct

6. Candor

A) Fallacious
B) Dishonest
C) Doctrine
D) Induce
E) Embezzle

7. Aloof

A) Interest
B) Aberration
C) Amoral
D) Confluence
E) Profuse

8. Dissuade

A) Vigilant
B) Savor
C) Persuade
D) Debunk
E) Fertile

9. Invigorate

A) Contempt
B) Erratic
C) Catastrophe
D) Dampen
E) Holistic

Answer Keys

1) E 2) A 3) D 4) D 5) B 6) B 7) A 8) C 9) D

1. **Lethargic** [luh-**thawr**-jik]
   adj syn: drowsy; dull.
   > The stifling classroom made Sarah *lethargic*; she felt as if she were about to sleep.

2. **Scourge** [skurj]
   noun def: a cause of affliction or calamity.
   > Disease and famine are *scourge* of humanity.

3. **Irascible** [ih-**ras**-uh-buhl]
   adj def: easily provoked to anger; very irritable. (**)
   > John saw an *irascible* old man walking by his house.

4. **Rancorous** [**rang**-ker-uhs]
   adj syn: expressing bitter; hostility. (**)
   > Many Americans are disgusted by recent political campaigns, which seem more *rancorous* than ever before.

5. **Improvident** [im-**prov**-i-duhnt]
   adj syn: without planning; foresight; negligent.
   > The *improvident* man spent all the money he received in his court settlement within two weeks.

6. **Convoluted** [**kon**-vuh-loo-tid]
   adj syn: twisting; complicated.
   > Tax law has become so *convoluted* that it is easy for people to accidentally violate it.

7. **Ostentatious** [os-ten-**tey**-shuhs]
   adj def: pretentious or conspicuous show to impress others. (**)
   > Lynn has been considered as an *ostentatious* dresser since she was little.

8. **Copious** [**koh**-pee-uhs]
   adj syn: abundant; plentiful.
   > The United Nation decided to provide a *copious* supply for the people in Japan.

9. **Clairvoyant** [klair-**voi**-uhnt]
   adj syn: psychic.
   > The *clairvoyant* fortuneteller claimed to have communicated with the ghost of Abraham Lincoln.

10. **Impeccable** [im-**pek**-uh-buhl]
    adj syn: flawless; no mistake. (**)
    > The crooks printed *impeccable* copies of the Super Bowl tickets, making it impossible to distinguish them from the real things.

11. **Matriculate** [muh-**trik**-yuh-leyt]
    verb def: enroll as a member of a college or university.
    > Since Suda-May *matriculates* at Harvard University this coming fall, she is going to have to move to Cambridge.

12. **Scrupulous** [**skroo**-pyuh-luhs]
    adj syn: restrained; honest; careful; precise. (***)
    > David could not have stolen Carmen's money; he is too *scrupulous* to do such a thing.

13. **Venerable** [**ven**-er-uh-buhl]
    adj syn: respected; reputation. (**)
    > In traditional Confucian society, the young treat their elders with *veneration*, deferring to the elder's wisdom.

14. **Gargantuan** [gahr-**gan**-choo-uhn]
    adj syn: huge; colossal.
    > The building Great Wall of China was one of the most *gargantuan* projects ever undertaken.

15. **Insurgent** [in-**sur**-juhnt]
    adj syn: rebellious.
    > Because the *insurgent* forces had occupied the capital and had gained control of the railway lines, several of war correspondents covering the uprising predicted a rebel victory.

16. **Sagacious** [suh-**gey**-shuhs]
    adj syn: discerning; wise. (**)
    > Only a leader as *sagacious* as Nelson Mandela could have united South Africa so successfully and peacefully.

17. **Jocular** [**jok**-yuh-ler]
    adj syn: joking; jesting; waggish.
    > Tim made *jocular* remarks about his teachers.

18. **Cynic** [**sin**-ik]
    noun def: person who distrusts the motives of others.
    > Have we become a nation of *cynics* who have lost faith in our own system of government?

19. **Affiliate** [uh-**fil**-ee-yet]
    verb def: to bring into close association.
    > The research center is *affiliated* with the university.

20. **Subterfuge** [**suhb**-ter-fyooj]
    noun syn: trick; tactic. (***)
    > Spies who are not skilled in the art of *subterfuge* are generally exposed before too long.

21. **Baleful** [**beyl**-fuhl]
    adj syn: harmful; detrimental. (**)
    > The sullen teenager gave his nagging mother a *baleful* look.

22. **Disdain** [dis-**deyn**]
    noun syn: contempt; scorn.
    > The millionaire was disliked by many people because she treated "little people" with such *disdain*.

23. **Incredulous** [in-**krej**-uh-luhs]
    adj syn: disinclined; indisposed; skeptical. (**)
    > He was *incredulous* as he listened to Ismael's wild fishing story about "the one that got away."

24. Impassive [im-**pas**-iv]
adj def: showing no emotion.

The King looked on *impassively* as the traitor argued desperately that his life should be spared.

25. Modicum [**mod**-i-kuhm]
noun def: s small amount, tiny. (***)

The plan for your new business is well designed; with a *modicum* luck, you should be successful.

26. Egregious [ih-**gree**-juhs]
adj syn: extraordinary; flagrant.

Steve was extremely shocked because his best friend was known as an *egregious* liar.

27. Munificent [myoo-**nif**-uh-suhnt]
adj syn: very generous; lavish.

The billion-dollar donation to the United Nation is probably the most *munificent* act of charity in history.

28. Gratuitous [gruh-**too**-i-uhs]
adj def: given freely. (**)

Who asked for your comment? We don't need any *gratuitous* criticism from someone has no business with us.

30. Capricious [kuh-**prish**-uhs]
adj syn: caprice; whim; erratic.

He is such a *capricious* businessman that I never know how he will react.

31. Charlatan [**shahr**-luh-tn]
noun syn: quack; fake.

"That *charlatan* prescribed the wrong medicine for me!" complained the patient.

32. Prerequisite [pri-**rek**-wuh-zit]
adj noun def: required beforehand. (***)
> A visa is still a *prerequisite* for travel in many countries.

33. Penchant [**pen**-chuhnt]
noun def: a strong inclination.
> Chris has a *penchant* for outdoor sports.

34. Culpable [**kuhl**-puh-buhl]
adj syn: guilty, responsible for wrong. (**)
> The CEO is *culpable* for the bankruptcy of the company; he was, after all, in charge of it.

35. Laconic [luh-**kon**-ik]
adj syn: brief and to the point.
> Many of the characters portrayed by Clint Eastwood are *laconic* types: strong man of few words.

36. Lugubrious [loo-**goo**-bree-uhs]
adj syn: sorrowful; mournful; dismal; gloomy.
> Irish wakes are a rousing departure from the *lugubrious* funeral services most people are accustomed to.

37. Verbose [ver-**bohs**]
adj syn: wordy; talkative.
> We had to make some major cuts in Senator Foghorn's speech because it was far too *verbose*.

38. Sonorous [suh-**nawr**-uhs]
adj def: producing a rich sound. (*)
> The *sonorous* blaring of the foghorn woke Lily up at 4:30 in the morning.

39. Lofty [**lawf**-tee]
adj def: very high.
> Barbara Jordan's fellow students used to tease her about her *lofty* ambition.

40. Impecunious [im-pi-**kyoo**-nee-uhs]

adj def: having no money. (*)

After the stock market crashed, many former millionaires found themselves *impecunious*

41. Prescience [**presh**-uhns]

noun syn: having foresight. (**)

Jonah's decision to sell the apartment turned out to be a *prescient* one, as its value soon dropped by half.

42. Predilection [pred-i-**ek**-shuhn]

noun syn: preference; tendency.

To relax from his presidential duties, Kennedy had a *predilection* for spy novels featuring James Bond.

43. Transitory [**tran**-si-tawr-ee]

adj def: quickly passing. (*)

Public moods tend to be *transitory*; people may be anxious and angry one month, but relatively content and optimistic the next.

44. Condescending [kon-duh-**sen**-ding]

adj def: showing an unusually patronizing descent from dignity. (****)

They resented the older neighbors' *condescending* cordiality.

45. Deleterious [del-**teer**-ee-uhs]

adj syn: harmful. (**)

About thirty years ago, scientists proved that working with asbestos could be *deleterious* to one's health, producing cancer and other diseases.

46. Cryptic [**krip**-tik]

adj syn: mysterious; hidden.

Martin loved to act mysterious, making *cryptic* comments no one could understand.

Synonym

1. Predilection
    A) Facility
    B) Tendency
    C) Exhume
    D) Egress
    E) Feasible

2. Lofty
    A) High
    B) Contravene
    C) Cadence
    D) Carnage
    E) Chromatic

3. Verbose
    A) Condolence
    B) Encumber
    C) Talkative
    D) Induce
    E) Embezzle

4. Culpable
    A) Endemic
    B) Extremity
    C) Blameful
    D) Egregious
    E) Elicit

5. Prerequisite

    A) Dispirit

    B) Dolorous

    C) Enthrall

    D) Necessary

    E) Verdict

6. Disdain

    A) Interloper

    B) Transit

    C) Reiterate

    D) Hydrate

    E) Disrespect

7. Cynic

    A) Sarcastic

    B) Infamy

    C) Imbue

    D) Intravenous

    E) Transitory

8. Egregious

    A) Penetrate

    B) Brevity

    C) Flagrant

    D) Acute

    E) Corpulence

Answer keys

1) B 2) A 3) C 4) C 5) D 6) E 7) A 8) C

Antonym

1. Deleterious
 A) Assisting
 B) Loquacious
 C) Delusion
 D) Elect
 E) Ablution

2. Transitory
 A) Placate
 B) Deportment
 C) Permanent
 D) Rapport
 E) Impotent

3. Impecunious
 A) Proximity
 B) Quaternary
 C) Pyre
 D) Protocol
 E) Rich

4. Laconic
 A) Query
 B) Philology
 C) Posit
 D) Talkative
 E) Premonition

5. Munificent
 A) Generous
 B) Mercy
 C) Quintessence
 D) Rectify
 E) Avarice

6. Modicum
    A) Centripetal
    B) Lot
    C) Pristine
    D) Impotent
    E) Provoke

7. Baleful
    A) Benefit
    B) Harmful
    C) Rectitude
    D) Primordial
    E) Xenophobia

8. Capricious
    A) Sporadic
    B) Disillusion
    C) Invariable
    D) Relentless
    E) Reproach

9. Impassive
    A) Polarize
    B) Censure
    C) Denude
    D) Fervent
    E) Savory

Answer keys

1) A 2) C 3) E 4) D 5) E 6) B 7) A 8) C 9) D

1. **Turgid** [**tur**-jid]
   adj def: swollen; distended; tumid
   > The story inclines to be too *turgid*, eccentric, and overwrought.

2. **Attest** [uh-**test**]
   verb syn: to bear witness; testify.
   > His works clearly *attest* his industry.

3. **Garrulous** [**gar**-uh-luhs]
   adj syn: very talkative. (*)
   > The *garrulous* parakeet distracted its owner with its
   > continuous talking.

4. **Tribunal** [trahy-**byoon**-l]
   noun def: a court of justice
   > He appeared before an honor *tribunal* only thirteen days later,
   > and in his opening statement confessed to all charges against him.

5. **Vainglorious** [veyn-**glawr**-ee-uh s]
   adj def: filled with or given to vainglory
   > He has always come across as deeply untrustworthy and
   > extremely *vainglorious*.

6. **Vilify** [**vil**-uh-fahy]
   verb syn: to speak ill of; defame; slander. (**)
   > The candidate *vilified* his opponent, accusing him of being
   > a wife-beating liar.

7. **Venue** [**ven**-yoo]
   noun def: the scene or locale of any action or event
   > The superstore also served as a *venue* for business meetings
   > with outsiders.

8. **Abysmal** [uh-**biz**-muhl]
   adj def: extremely or hopelessly bad.
   > Steve has been suffering from *abysmal* poverty since his business
   > went bankrupt.

9. **Vertigo** [**vul**-ti-goh]
   noun def: a dizzying sensation of tilting within stable surrounding
   For the doctor, it was a trick on the inner ear, an amusing
   exercise in *vertigo*.

10. **Insubstantial** [in-suhb-**stan**-shuhl]
    adj syn: modest; insignificant. (***)
    The losses we risk are *insubstantial* compared with the massive
    profits we stand to gain.

11. **Disseminate** [dih-**sem**-uh-meyt]
    verb syn: to scatter or spread widely.
    He tried not to *disseminate* information about preventive medicine.

12. **Improvident** [im-**prov**-i-duhnt]
    adj syn: without planning or foresight; negligent.
    The *improvident* woman spent all the money she received in
    her court settlement within two weeks.

13. **Subvert** [suhb-**vurt**]
    verb syn: undermine; corrupt. (**)
    The traitor intended to *subvert* loyal citizens of the crown with
    the revolutionary propaganda he distributed.

14. **Impudence** [**im**-pyuh-duhns]
    noun syn: impertinence; insolence. (****)
    When kissed on the cheek by a perfect stranger, Lady Catherine
    exclaimed," Of all the nerve! Young man, I should have you
    horsewhipped for your *impudence*.

15. **Touchy** [**tuhch**-ee]
    adj def: apt to take offense on sight
    It always seems a little *touchy* asking about salaries prior to the nod.

16. Abrogate [ab-ruh-geyt]
verb syn: abolish; annul. (**)
> The governor made a solid determination to *abrogate* the laws enacted last year.

17. Exhort [ig-zawrt]
verb def: to urge or incite by strong appeals. (**)
> Rob's friends *exhorted* him to beware of ice on the roads when insisted on driving home in the middle of a snowstorm.

18. Reproach [ri-prohch]
verb syn: to find fault; blame.
> Renee *reproached* her boyfriend for forgetting to buy her a Christmas present.

19. Agrarian [uh-grair-ee-uhn]
adj def: relating to farming or rural matters. (**)
> Charles took a course in *agrarian* accounting in order to help his family run the farm after college.

20. Respite [res-pit]
noun def: interval of relief.
> The brief *respite* was over; once again, Bo's phone was ringing off the hook with customer complaints.

21. Turpitude [tur-pi-tood]
noun syn: vile; shameful.
> The priest's affair with the teenage parishioner was considered an act of *turpitude*.

22. Perspicacity [pur-spi-kas-i-tees]
noun def: keenness of observation or understanding.
> Journalist Murray Kempton was famous for the *perspicacity* of his comments on social and political issues.

23. Metamorphosis [met-uh-**mawr**-fuh-sis]
noun syn: change; transformation. (**)
The *metamorphosis* of a caterpillar into a butterfly is a fascinating process.

24. Goad [gohd]
verb syn: prod; urge. (*)
Denise *goaded* her sister Leigh into running the marathon with her.

25. Demur [dih-**mur**]
verb syn: to doubt; objections. (**)
They wanted to make him the treasurer, but he *demurred*.

26. Invective [in-**vek**-tiv]
noun syn: censure; reproach.
A stream of *invective* poured from Mrs. Pratt's mouth as she watched the vandals smash her ceramic frog.

27. Irrelevant [ih-**rel**-uh-vuhnt]
adj syn: not applicable; pertinent.
His lecture often strays to interesting but *irrelevant* subjects.

28. Affinity [uh-**fin**-i-tee]
noun syn: fondness; liking; similarity. (***)
George felt an instant *affinity* for his new neighbor when he realized that he, too, was a Bronco's fan.

29. Wisp [wisp]
noun def: a thin strip or fragment
Wisps of steam rose up from the teapot.

30. Debunk [dih-**buhngk**]
verb def: to expose as false or worthless. (**)
The magician loves to *debunk* psychics, mediums, clairvoyants, and others who claim supernatural power.

31. Vulpine [**vuhl**-pahyn]

adj def: of or resembling fox; cunning or crafty

Having made a joke, he would smile in his beard with a sort of *vulpine* pleasure which was quite unaffected by anyone else's reactions.

32. Mendacious [men-**dey**-shuhs]

adj syn: false; dishonest. (***)

So many of her stories were *mendacious* that I decided she must be a pathological liar.

33. Disdain [dis-**deyn**]

noun syn: contempt; scorn. (**)

The millionaire was disliked by many people because she treated "little people" with such *disdain*.

34. Extol [ik-**stohl**]

verb syn: to praise highly; laud. (*)

She always *extols* the beauty of Naples.

35. Waggish [**wag**-ish]

adj def: roguish in merriment and good humor

A *waggish* disposition that often got him into trouble as a child.

36. Incongruous [in-**kong**-groo-uhs]

adj syn: not fitting; absurd.

Dave saw nothing *incongruous* about wearing sneakers with his tuxedo; he could not understand why his date took one look at him and started to laugh.

37. Predilection [pred-l-**ek**-shuhn]

noun syn: a liking; preference.

To relax from his presidential duties, Kennedy had a *predilection* for spy novels featuring James Bond.

38. Entail [en-**teyl**]

verb def: to impose as a burden. (**)

It is said that success *entails* hard work.

39. Vintner [vint-ner]
    noun def: a person who makes wine or sells
        Patience was a virtue, especially among *vintners*.
                    -Neal Stephenson, et. al., "Dreamer"

40. Pedantic [puh-**dan**-tik]
    adj def: showing off learning. (***)
        Leavening his decisions with humorous, down-to-earth anecdotes,
        Judge Wagner was a pleasant contrast to the typical *pedantic*
        legal scholar.

41. Unassailable [uhn-uh-**sey**-luh-buh l]
    adj def: not open to attack or assault
        "On the other hand the truth of the thoughts communicated
        here seems to me *unassailable* and definitive"
            -Wittgenstein's Tractatus Logico-Philosophicus Preface

42. Exuberant [ig-**zoo**-ber-uhnt]
    adj def: widely joyous. (**)
        As the final seconds of the game ticked away, the fans of
        the winning team began an *exuberant* celebration.

43. Unearthly [uhn-**urth**-lee]
    adj def: seeming not to belong to this earth
        Those qualities have created an almost *unearthly* landscape that is
        as beautiful as it is desolate.

44. Tutelage [**toot**-l-ij]
    noun def: the act of guarding, protecting, or guiding
        Many students went on to establish successful careers under
        his *tutelage*.

45. Apprehend [ap-ri-**hend**]
    verb def: to take into custody; arrest by legal warrant. (**)
        The police *apprehended* the burglar.

Synonym

1. Exuberant
A) Valid
B) Energetic
C) Intrepid
D) Verbiage
E) Aversion

2. Pragmatic
A) Practical
B) Utopia
C) Hypothermia
D) Perturbation
E) Urbane

3. Pedantic
A) Contentious
B) Apotheosis
C) Timorous
D) Academic
E) Adumbrate

4. Predilection
A) Umbrage
B) Verisimilitude
C) Tendency
D) Venue
E) Veracious

5. Invective

A) Despair
B) Transpire
C) Astringent
D) Subsequent
E) Accuse

6. Perpetuate

A) Detest
B) Aver
C) Avert
D) Revert
E) Last

7. Disseminate

A) Spread
B) Torpid
C) Torpor
D) Tensile
E) Evacuate

8. Prolific

A) Inebriate
B) Productive
C) Dispense
D) Bias
E) Insolence

Answer keys

1) B   2) A   3) D   4) C   5) E   6) E   7) A   8) B

Antonym

1. Unearthly
- A) Natural
- B) Ambivalent
- C) Intervene
- D) Tortuous
- E) Versatile

2. Disdain
- A) Retrospect
- B) Sophomoric
- C) Respect
- D) Assonance
- E) Aspersion

3. Extol
- A) Inscribe
- B) Blame
- C) Testament
- D) Utopia
- E) Extort

4. Sparse
- A) Sonorous
- B) Plentiful
- C) Rupture
- D) Secede
- E) Sedition

5. Respite
- A) Construe
- B) Sentient
- C) Obloquy
- D) Supercilious
- E) Continuation

6. Reproach
    A) Rudimentary
    B) Arrogant
    C) Seminal
    D) Extol
    E) Subsequent

7. Exhort
    A) Encourage
    B) Discourage
    C) Stricture
    D) Assent
    E) Designation

8. Vilify
    A) Reverent
    B) Edify
    C) Eulogize
    D) Indict
    E) Abstruse

9. Insipid
    A) Interesting
    B) Perpetuate
    C) Vague
    D) Winsome
    E) Inadequate

Answer keys

1) A 2) C 3) B 4) B 5) E 6) D 7) B 8) C 9) A

1. **Indeterminate** [in-di-**tur**-muh-nit]
   adj def: not precisely fixed in extent; indefinite; uncertain
   > In those days every state in the country had a system of
   > *indeterminate* prison sentences.

2. **Parochial** [puh-**roh**-kee-uhl]
   adj def: limited, narrow in scope. (**)
   > David showed *parochial* views toward Korean English education.

3. **Intractable** [in-**trak**-tuh-buhl]
   adj syn: hard to treat, relieve, or cure.
   > Tim appeared to have an *intractable* pain in his leg.

4. **Diffident** [**dif**-i-duhnt]
   adj syn: timid; shy.
   > Some with a *diffident* personality should pursue a career that
   > involves little public contact.

5. **Holistic** [hoh-**lis**-tik]
   adj def: emphasizing importance of the whole and independence
   >   of its part. (**)
   > Angie is studying internal medicine and believes in a *holistic*
   > approach to healing.

6. **Catharsis** [kuh-**thar**-sis]
   noun syn: purifying; cleansing.
   > Plays can be more satisfying if they end in some part of
   > emotional *catharsis* for the characters involved.

7. **Treacherous** [**trech**-er-uhs]
   adj syn: untrustworthy; disloyal.
   > Nazi Germany provided to be a *treacherous* ally, first signing
   > a peace pact with the Soviet Union, then invading.

8. **Enchant** [en-**chant**]
   verb def: to subject to magical influence; bewitch. (**)
   > Fairytales about witches who *enchant* handsome princess and
   > beautiful maidens capture Jessica's attention.

9. **Revulsion** [ri-**vuhl**-shuhn]
    noun syn: a strong feeling of repugnance; dislike.
    Cruelty fills me with *revulsion*.

10. **Bewilder** [bih-**wil**-der]
    verb def: to confuse or puzzle completely; perplex.
    These shifting attitudes *bewilder* me.

11. **Speculation** [spek-yuh-**ley**-shuhn]
    noun def: a conclusion or position reached by such contemplation. (***)
    These *speculations* are impossible to verify.

12. **Primordial** [prahy-**mawr**-dee-uhl]
    adj def: original, existing from the beginning.
    The first organisms were formed eons ago from *primordial* ooze.

13. **Plausible** [**plaw**-zuh-buhl]
    adj syn: apparently believable.
    The idea that a widespread conspiracy to kill President Kennedy
    has been kept secret for over thirty years hardly seems *plausible*.

14. **Curtail** [ker-**teyl**]
    verb syn: to shorten. (**)
    Because of the military emergency, all soldiers on leave were
    ordered to *curtail* their absences and return to duty.

15. **Raze** [reyz]
    verb syn: to tear down; demolish.
    The mayor of the city decided to *raze* a row of old buildings.

16. **Corroborate** [kuh-**rob**-uh-reyt]
    verb adj syn: supporting with evidence; confirming. (**)
    A passerby who had witnessed the crime gave *corroborating*
    testimony about the presence of the accused person.

17. Indispensable [in-di-**spen**-shu-buhl]
adj syn: absolute; necessary; essential. (***)
> Bill has been known as an *indispensable* member of staff.

18. Pinnacle [**pin**-uh-kuhl]
noun def: the highest or culminating point. (**)
> William has reached the *pinnacle* of his SAT teaching career.

19. Nadir [**ney**-der]
noun def: lowest point.
> As Lou waited in line to audition for the diaper commercial, he realized he had reached the *nadir* of his acting career.

20. Paradigm [**par**-uh-dahym]
noun syn: ideal example; model. (*)
> The ribs restaurant owner used McDonald's as a *paradigm* for the expansion of his business.

21. Inception [in-**sep**-shuhn]
noun syn: beginning. (***)
> Even from its *inception*, those who were involved in the plan knew that it probably wouldn't succeed.

22. Periphery [puh-**rif**-uh-ree]
noun syn: the relatively minor; irrelevant.
> The preliminary research did not, of course, take me beyond the *periphery* of my problem.

23. Detrimental [de-truh-**men**-tl]
adj syn: causing damaging; harmful. (**)
> Eating sugar too much has a *detrimental* affect on health.

24. Salutary [**sal**-yuh-ter-ee]
adj syn: favorable; promoting. (*)
> Exercising everyday will have *salutary* effect on losing weight.

25. Permeate [**pur**-mee-yet]
verb syn: to spread through; penetrate. (***)

Little by little, the smell of gas from the broken pipe *permeated* the house.

26. Recluse [**rek**-loos]
adj def: a person who lives in seclusion or apart from society. (**)

During the last years of her life, actress Greta Garbo led a *reclusive* existence, rarely appearing in public.

27. Disaffected [dis-uh-**fek**-tid]
adj syn: discontented; disloyal. (***)

The *disaffected* employee spent most of his time at work surfing the Web for job opportunities and sending out resumes.

28. Ascetic [uh-**set**-ik]
adj def: practicing strict self-discipline from moral or spiritual reasons.

The so-called Desert Fathers were hermits who lived an *ascetic* life of fasting, study, and prayer.

29. Punitive [**pyoo**-ni-tiv]
adj def: having to do with punishment.

The teacher banished Jack from the classroom as a *punitive* measure, but the boy was actually overjoyed to be missing class.

30. Poignant [**poin**-yuhnt]
adj syn: pungent to the smell; bitter. (**)

John smelt something *poignant* as soon as he walked into the restaurant.

31. Parsimony [pahr-**suh**-moh-nee]
noun syn: excessive economy; frugality. (*)

Ethel gained a reputation for *parsimony* when she refused to pay for her daughter's college education.

32. Ineffable [in-ef-uh-buhl]
adj def: incapable of being expressed or described in words.
>   The doctor prescribed an *ineffable* medicine, which is supposed to induce a lowering of the blood pressure.

33. Exorbitant [ig-zawr-bi-tuhnt]
adj def: exceeding the bounds of custom, propriety. (***)
>   The owner of the store charged his clients an *exorbitant* price.

34. Dubious [doo-bee-uhs]
adj syn: doubtful.
>   Despite the chairman's attempts to convince the committee members that his plan would succeed, most of them remained *dubious*.

35. Intuitive [in-too-i-tiv]
adj def: known directly.
>   An experienced card player sometimes has to protect oneself from *intuitive* searches by the casino police.

36. Disconcert [dis-kuhn-surt]
verb syn: to confuse; embarrass. (*)
>   When the hallway bells began to ring halfway through her lecture, the speaker was *disconcerted* and didn't know what to do.

37. Rudimentary [roo-duh-men-tuh-ee]
adj syn: first principles. (**)
>   In order to speak English well, a language learner must have a *rudimentary* knowledge of written English grammar.

38. Intransigent [in-tran-si-juhnt]
adj syn: uncompromising; refusing. (**)
>   The professor was *intransigent* on the deadline, insisting that everyone turn the assignment in on Friday.

39. Energize [en-er-jahyz]
verb syn: to give energy.

Alex tried to *energize* the spirit with brave words.

40. Desecrate [des-i-kreyt]
verb def: to abuse something sacred. (**)

The archaeologist tried to explain to the explorer that he had *desecrated* the temple by spitting in it, but to no avail.

41. Hypothermia [hahy-puh-**thur**-mee-uh]
noun def: subnormal body temperature.

The Arctic explorer, suffering from *hypothermia,* was wrapped in thick blankets by his companions.

42. Blandish [**blan**-dish]
verb syn: flatter; cajole; coax. (**)

We *blandished* the bouncer with compliments until he finally let us into the club.

43. Precipitate [pri-**sip**-i-teyt]
verb def: to throw down from the height.

It is fairly certain that Lloyd's incessant smoking *precipitated* early death from cancer.

44. Querulous [**kwer**-uh-luhs]
adj syn: full of complaints. (***)

Her friends were annoyed with her constantly *querulous* behavior.

45. Dejected [dih-**jek**-tid]
adj syn: disheartened; low-spirited.

The *dejected* expression on the face of the loser spoiled my victory.

Synonym

1. Querulous
>A) Complain
>B) Ambulatory
>C) Anarchy
>D) Accretion
>E) Attest

2. Blandish
>A) Anesthetic
>B) Abscond
>C) Flatter
>D) Annul
>E) Acerbic

3. Rudimentary
>A) Altruism
>B) Basic
>C) Amiable
>D) Perambulator
>E) Animosity

4. Intransigent
>A) Misanthrope
>B) Autonomous
>C) Aspersion
>D) Uncompromising
>E) Antipathy

5. Disconcert
    A) Anomaly
    B) Absolve
    C) Allure
    D) Diffident
    E) Agitate

6. Disaffected
    A) Diffract
    B) Disloyal
    C) Confluence
    D) Infusion
    E) Progeny

7. Pinnacle
    A) Discursive
    B) Indolent
    C) Crest
    D) Effervescent
    E) Foreboding

8. Parochial
    A) Narrow
    B) Epidemic
    C) Render
    D) Succulent
    E) Redolent

Answer keys

1) A 2) C 3) B 4) D 5) E 6) B 7) C 8) A

Antonym

1. Dejected
A) Induct
B) Joyous
C) Doleful
D) Diffuse
E) Viaduct

2. Desecrate
A) Honor
B) Credulous
C) Monochrome
D) Regicide
E) Cursory

3. Energize
A) Disburse
B) Cascade
C) Enervate
D) Decapitate
E) Carnal

4. Dubious
A) Entice
B) Eulogy
C) Disparage
D) Decathlon
E) Certain

5. Parsimony
A) Economy
B) Empathy
C) Squandering
D) Entreat
E) Devoid

6. Detrimental
- A) Harmful
- B) Beneficial
- C) Convoke
- D) Autocrat
- E) Credence

7. Corroborate
- A) Refute
- B) Confirm
- C) Diatribe
- D) Corporeal
- E) Incredulous

8. Revulsion
- A) Outstrip
- B) Aggrandize
- C) Energize
- D) Penchant
- E) Demure

9. Curtail
- A) Aspersion
- B) Underscore
- C) Lengthen
- D) Provocative
- E) Sedition

Answer keys

1) B 2) A 3) C 4) E 5) C 6) B 7) A 8) D 9) C

1. **Jubilant** [**joo**-buh-luhnt]
   adj def: showing great enjoy. syn: satisfaction.
   The cheers of the *jubilant* victors; the *jubilant* climax of
   his symphony.

2. **Outlandish** [out-**lan**-dish]
   adj syn: strange; odd. (*)
   Kim sometimes wears *outlandish* clothes.

3. **Hidebound** [**hahyd**-bound]
   adj def: excessively rigid; dry and stiff.
   The *hidebound* old patriarch would not tolerate any opposition
   to his order.

4. **Mundane** [muhn-**deyn**]
   adj syn: worldly; earthly. (***)
   The plot of that thriller was completely *mundane*; as usual, the film
   ended in a huge explosion.

5. **Depreciate** [dih-**pree**-shee-yet]
   verb def: to reduce the value.
   Alex attempted to *depreciate* the value of the shoes in order for
   the salesperson to offer him a better price.

6. **Invigorate** [in-**vig**-uh-reyt]
   verb syn: to give energy; to stimulate. (**)
   As her car climbed the mountain road, Lucinda felt *invigorated* by
   the clear air and the cool breezes.

7. **Lugubrious** [loo-**goo**-bree-uhs]
   adj syn: mournful; dismal.
   Listening to the *lugubrious* song of lost love appeared to make
   the listeners cry.

8. **Soporific** [sop-uh-**rif**-ik]
   adj def: tending to cause asleep. (**)
   This movie proved to be so *soporific* that soon loud snores were
   heard throughout the theater.

9. Latent [leyt-nt]
adj def: the state of being dormant.

Milton's *latent* paranoia began to emerge as he was put under more and more stress at the office.

10. Compliance [kuhm-**plahy**-uhn-see]
noun syn: obeying.

Steve was born with a *compliance* nature to his boss.

11. Discretion [dih-**skresh**-uhn]
noun def: the power or right to decide.

It is entirely within my *discretion* whether I will go or stay.

12. Hypochondria [hahy-puh-**kon**-dree-uh]
noun def: unfounded belief that one is often ill.

Dr. Pradesh groaned when he saw Mr. Copper on his appointment list yet again; the man was a classic victim of *hypochondria*.

13. Partisan [**pahr**-tuh-zuhn]
adj def: reflecting strong allegiance to a particular party.

The vote on the president's budget was strictly *partisan*: every member of the president's party voted yes, and all others voted no.

14. Impassive [im-**pas**-iv]
adj def: showing no emotion. (**)

Elizabeth remained *impassive* as a military officer informed her of her son's death.

15. Burgeon [**bur**-juhn]
verb syn: to grow; develop. (***)

He *burgeoned* into a fine actor.

16. Wane [weyn]
verb def: to decrease in strength; intensity. (***)

Her enthusiasm for the cause is *waning*.

17. **Attenuate** [uh-**ten**-yoo-yet]
    verb syn: to weaken; reduce. (**)
        His continuous failures slowly *attenuated* his long-term desire
        to go back to school.

18. **Depravity** [dih-**prav**-i-tee]
    noun syn: sinfulness; immoral.
        The *depravity* of actor's Hollywood lifestyle shocked his
        traditional parents.

19. **Conflate** [kuhn-**fleyt**]
    verb def: to fuse into one entity.
        Jessica *conflated* dissenting voices into one protest.

20. **Benighted** [bih-**nahy**-tid]
    adj syn: unenlightened. (*)
        Ben scoffed at the crowd, as he believed it consisted entirely of
        benighted individuals.

21. **Surfeit** [**sur**-fit]
    noun syn: to excess. (**)
        Most American families have a *surfeit* of food and drink on
        Thanksgiving Day.

22. **Mendacious** [men-**dey**-shuhs]
    adj syn: false. (***)
        So many of her stories were *mendacious* that I decided she must
        be a pathological liar.

23. **Substantiate** [suhb-**stan**-shee-yet]
    verb syn: to prove.
        Alice *substantiated* an idea through action.

24. **Buttress** [**buh**-tris]
    noun def: something that supports and strengthens. (**)
        The endorsement of the American Medical Association is a
        powerful *buttress* for the claims made about this new medicine.

25. Superficial [soo-per-fish-uhl]

adj syn: hasty; shallow; phony.

The politician was friendly, but in a *superficial,* unconvincing kind of way.

26. Profuse [pruh-fyoos]

adj syn: lavish; extravagant.

Janet gave *profuse* apologies for being unable to arrive at the meeting.

27. Stagnate [stag-neyt]

verb def: to become stale. (*)

Having had no contact with the outside world for generation, African culture gradually *stagnated.*

28. Piebald [pahy-bawld]

adj def: having matches of black and white

Occasionally, you may see an all-white or a *piebald* deer, which are simply color variations of the species.

29. Tenacity [tuh-nas-i-tee]

noun syn: firmness. (***)

Jean could not believe that *tenacity* of Inspector Javert.

30. Illusory [ih-loo-suh-ree]

adj syn: deceptive.

The costs of running the lemonade stand were so high that Tom's profit proved *illusory.*

31. Enliven [en-lahy-vuhn]

verb def: to make vigorous. (**)

The wit of Mencken *enlivened* his age.

32. Flippant [flip-uhnt]

adj syn: disrespectful; shallow.

The audience was shocked by his *flippant* remarks about patriotism.

33. Vicissitude [vi-**sis**-i-tood]

noun syn: a change; alternation. (***)

They remained friends through the *vicissitudes* of 40 years

34. Lien [lee-**uhn**]

noun def: right to possess.

The bank took a *lien* on the leader's house to protect itself in case he defaulted on his loan.

35. Malediction [mal-i-**dik**-shuhn]

noun syn: curse.

In the fairy tale "Sleeping Beauty," the princess is trapped in a death-like sleep because of the *malediction* uttered by an angry witch.

36. Tenet [**ten**-it]

noun syn: belief; doctrine. (**)

One of the *tenets* of the Muslim religion is that eating pork is not acceptable.

37. Sordid [**sawr**-did]

adj syn: filthy; contemptible.

Jason has spent ten years living in a *sordid* house.

38. Gratuitous [gruh-**too**-i-uhs]

adj def: given freely. (*)

Since her opinion was not requested, her harsh criticism of his singing seemed a *gratuitous* insult.

39. Munition [myoo-**nish**-uhn]

noun syn: ammunition.

Soon after the *munitions* plant was blown up, the troops ran out of ammunition and surrendered.

40. Vicarious [vahy-**kair**-ee-uhs]
adj syn: indirect. (***)
Jane learned a lot of valuable things through *vicarious* experiences.

41. Hackneyed [**hak**-need]
adj def: worn out by overuse. (**)
We always mock my father for his *hackneyed* expressions and dated hairstyle.

42. Spawn [spawn]
verb syn: to generate; produce. (**)
The frog *spawned* hundreds of tadpoles.

43. Sanctimonious [sangk-tuh-**moh**-nee-uhs]
adj syn: showing false.
The *sanctimonious* prayers of the TV preacher were interspersed with requests that the viewers send him money.

44. Bucolic [byoo-**kol**-ik]
adj syn: pastoral; rural.
Sophia used to enjoy an idyllic *bucolic* life.

45. Invincible [in-vin-sub-buhl]
adj def: impossible to conquer.
For three years at the height of his career, boxer Mike Tyson seemed *invincible*.

> " *This book is awesome. I purchased this right before the real SAT test. It was tremendously helpful. Each word has a concrete example sentence that helps me understand the definition of the word easily.* "

Stella Sim *(River Dell Regional High School)*

Synonym

1. Spawn
  A) Epidemic
  B) Generate
  C) Demagogue
  D) Quotidian
  E) Diatribe

2. Sordid
  A) Filthy
  B) Retrograde
  C) Digress
  D) Epigraph
  E) Gratitude

3. Flippant
  A) Colloquy
  B) Pellucid
  C) Manual
  D) Disrespectful
  E) Misanthrope

4. Profuse
  A) Itinerant
  B) Interject
  C) Excessive
  D) Catholic
  E) Heterodox

5. Mendacious

    A) Aggregate

    B) Egregious

    C) Hapless

    D) False

    E) Mishap

6. Attenuate

    A) Adjunct

    B) Bonhomie

    C) Weaken

    D) Intermittent

    E) Intrinsic

7. Impassive

    A) Aloof

    B) Bilateral

    C) Abject

    D) Conjugal

    E) Perjure

8. Outlandish

    A) Refraction

    B) Foreign

    C) Aggravate

    D) Enliven

    E) Toil

Answer keys

1) B   2) A   3) D   4) C   5) D   6) C   7) A   8) B

Antonym

1. Hackneyed

    A) Original
    B) Shallow
    C) Condemned
    D) Amazing
    E) Voracious

2. Malediction

    A) Capricious
    B) Superfluous
    C) Blessing
    D) Prodigal
    E) Enmity

3. Tenacity

    A) Proximity
    B) Ineptness
    C) Beneficence
    D) Partisanship
    E) Magnanimity

4. Superficial

    A) Greedy
    B) Social
    C) Cunning
    D) Careful
    E) Hardy

5. Surfeit

    A) Aggressive
    B) Repudiate
    C) Jingoistic
    D) Undermine
    E) Need

6. Wane
A) Wavering
B) Increase
C) Assuage
D) Reconcile
E) Dogmatic

7. Lugubrious
A) Happiness
B) Polemical
C) Stipulate
D) Contemplate
E) Surmise

8. Compliancy
A) Fickle
B) Gauche
C) Vigilant
D) Disobey
D) Futile

9. Buttress
A) Ambivalent
B) Clumsy
C) Weaken
D) Esoteric
E) Impenetrable

Answer keys

1) A 2) C 3) B 4) D 5) E 6) B 7) A 8) D 9) C

1. **Bustle** [**buhs**-uhl]
   noun syn: commotion; energetic activity.
   The *bustle* of the crowd made Andrea remember how much she hated Christmas shopping.

2. **Portend** [**pawr**-tend]
   verb syn: to indicate a future. (*)
   According to folklore, a red sky at dawn *portends* a day of stormy weather.

3. **Tedium** [**tee**-dee-uhm]
   noun syn: boredom; tiresome. (**)
   For most people, watching the Weather Channel for 24 hours would be sheer *tedium*.

4. **Blight** [blahyt]
   verb syn: to afflict; to destroy. (***)
   The farmers feared that the previous night's frost had *blighted* the potato crops entirely.

5. **Prodigal** [**prod**-i-guhl]
   adj def: wastefully or recklessly extravagant. (****)
   Don't be so *prodigal* spending my money; when you have earned some money, you can waste it as much as you want.

6. **Hoard** [hawrd]
   verb def: accumulate for preservation.
   Tim always tried to *hoard* food during shortage.

7. **Soothe** [sooth]
   verb syn: to tranquilize; calm.
   Joyce *soothed* his boyfriend with a hot drink.

8. **Adamant** [**ad**-uh-muhnt]
   adj syn: uncompromising. (***)
   The lawyer was *adamant* in his tireless defense of the death penalty.

9. Chastise [**chas**-tahyz]
verb syn: to discipline; criticize severely.
> The king decided to *chastise* a thief by corporal punishment.

10. Impugn [im-**pyoon**]
verb syn: to challenge as false.
> "How dare you *impugn* my honorable motives?" protested the lawyer on being accused of ambulance chasing.

11. Denounce [dih-**nouns**]
verb syn: to condemn; censure. (**)
> People *denounced* a politician as morally corrupt.

12. Delectable [dih-**lek**-tuh-buhl]
adj syn: delightful; highly pleasing.
> Kenny enjoyed a *delectable* dinner fixed by his wife.

13. Palliate [**pal**-ee-eyt]
verb syn: to make less serious; ease. (*)
> The accused's crime was so vicious that the defense lawyer could not *palliate* it for the jury.

14. Compulsive [kuhm-**puhl**-siv]
adj syn: obsessive; fanatic.
> A *compulsive* liar, Paul told his boss that he had once climbed Mount Everest with a yak on his back.

15. Felicitous [fi-**lis**-i-tuhs]
adj syn: pleasing; fortunate. (***)
> The sudden blossoming of the dogwood trees on the morning of Matt's wedding seemed a *felicitous* sign of good luck.

16. Expiate [**ek**-spee-eyt]
verb syn: to atone for; make amends for.
> The president's apology to the survivors of the notorious Tuskegee experiments was his attempt to *expiate* the nation's guilt over their mistreatment.

17. Expropriate [eks-**proh**-pree-yet]
verb def: to seize ownership. (**)
> When the communists came to power in China, they *expropriated* most of the businesses and turned them over to government-appointed managers.

18. Fractious [**frak**-shuhs]
adj syn: troublesome; unruly. (***)
> Members of British Parliament are often *fractious*, shouting insults and caused by several fortuitous trend.

19. Paucity [**paw**-si-tee]
noun def: smallness of quantity; scarcity.
> The country has a *paucity* of natural resources.

20. Preamble [pree-**am**-buhl]
noun def: an introductory statement.
> The *preamble* to the Constitution begins with the famous words, "We the people of the United States of America."

21. Abridge [uh-**brij**]
verb syn: to condense; shorten.
> The teacher assigned an *abridged* version of Tristram Shandy to her class, as the original was very long.

22. Serenity [suh-**ren**-i-tee]
noun syn: calmness; peacefulness. (**)
> Lynette's meditation helps her to achieve true *serenity*.

23. Stoic [**stoh**-ik]
adj def: showing little feeling (**)
> A soldier must respond to the death of comrades in *stoic* fashion, since the fighting will not stop for his grief.

24. Imperious [im-**peer**-ee-uhs]
adj def: arrogantly self-assured.

The *imperious* princess demanded that her servants do back flips every time they came into her presence.

25. Incisive [in-**sahy**-siv]
adj syn: perceptive; penetrating.

The psychologist's *incisive* analysis of her patient's childhood helped him to understand his own behavior.

26. Capitulate [kuh-**pich**-uh-leyt]
verb syn: to submit completely. (**)

After atom bombs devastated Hiroshima and Nagasaki, the Japanese had little choice but to *capitulate*.

27. Acrimonious [ak-ruh-**moh**-nee-uhs]
adj syn: biting; harsh; caustic.

The election campaign became *acrimonious*, as the candidates traded insults and accusations.

28. Sycophant [**sik**-uh-fahnt]
noun syn: yes-man; self-serving flatterer, obsequious. (***)

Dreading criticism, the actor surrounded himself with admirers and *sycophants*.

29. Complement [**kom**-pluh-muhnt]
noun def: something that completes or makes perfect.

A good wine is a *complement* to a good meal.

30. Recalcitrant [ri-**kal**-si-truhnt]
adj def: resisting authority or control. (***)

The *recalcitrant* mule refused to go down the treacherous path, even when its master pulled at its reins.

31. Castigate [kas-ti-geyt]
verb syn: to punish; chastise. (**)
> Authorities in Singapore harshly *castigate* perpetrators of what would be considered minors crimes in the United States.

32. Ostracize [os-truh-sahyz]
verb def: to exclude from a group.
> In Bible times, those who suffered from the disease of leprosy were *ostracized* and forced to live alone.

33. Unwitting [uhn-wit-ing]
adj syn: unintentional; inadvertent; accidental. (***)
> Not looking where she was going, Jane charged into the subway car, *unwittingly* knocking down a blind man.

34. Adversity [ad-vur-si-tee]
noun syn: misfortune.
> It is easy to be patient and generous when things are going well; a person's true character is revealed under *adversity.*

35. Belabor [bih-ley-bor]
verb syn: to explain; worry about. (*)
> He kept *belaboring* the point long after we had agreed.

36. Dire [dahr-uhr]
adj syn: causing or involving great fear.
> An increasing number of economists made *dire* prediction about the stock market.

37. Apathy [ap-uh-thee]
noun def: lack of feeling or emotion. (**)
> The *apathy* of voters is so great that less than half the people who are eligible to vote bother to do so.

38. Empathy [em-puh-thee]

noun def: vicarious experiencing of the feelings.

By means of *empathy*, a great painting becomes a mirror of the self.

39. Synopsis [si-nop-sis]

noun def: brief or condensed statement.

The methods used in the experiment were a *synopsis* of techniques taken from biology and medicine.

40. Nonchalant [non-shuh-lahnt]

adj def: appearing to be unconcerned. (***)

Unlike the other players on the football team, who pumped their fists when their names were announced, John ran on the field with a *nonchalant* wave.

41. Exalt [ig-zawlt]

verb syn: to raise in rank; honor. (**)

He was *exalted* to the position of president.

42. Novice [nov-is]

noun syn: beginner; tyro. (*)

Lifting your head before you finish your swing is a typical mistake committed by the *novice* at golf.

43. Espouse [ih-spouz]

verb syn: to support; to advocate. (**)

Due to his religious belief, the preacher could not *espouse* the practice of abortion.

44. Polarize [poh-luh-rahyz]

verb def: to divide into sharply opposing factions. (*)

The controversy has *polarized* voters into pro-abortion and anti-abortion groups.

45. Metaphor [met-uh-fawr]

noun def: figure of speech comparing two things.

The *metaphor* "a sea of troubles" suggests a lot of troubles by comparing their number to the vastness of the sea.

46. Ruthless [rooth-lis]

adj syn: cruel; merciless.

Hitler is known as the most *ruthless* tyrant in world history.

❝ Mastering Core SAT Words *really helps me memorize the SAT words. Its drill section and appendix are especially helpful in reminding me of the words I memorized and imprinting them on my memory permanently. With* Mastering Core SAT Words, *I not only get to do well on the SAT vocabulary section but I also get to use some fancy words in my papers.* **❞**

Alice Lee *(Northern Valley Regional Demarest High School)*

" *Having known Mr. Shin for a few years I was already expecting a lot from his new book,* Mastering Core SAT Words. *However, when I actually saw the book, I realized my expectation was not high enough to compare with this book. Having looked at many other SAT vocabulary books, I discovered that this book was very detailed and organized and allowed me to study with simplicity. This book is sure to help you memorize vocabulary for your SAT test.* "

Alex Yang *(Leonia High School)*
Admitted to St. John's and Rutgers University, Business

" Mastering Core SAT Words *is a great tool to use to boost your score for the Critical Reading section of the SAT. It not only helped my score go up but it also enhanced my vocabulary. As I flipped through pages, I was surprised to find numerous words that I had troubles with during the exam in March. This book contains the essential words that have appeared in the past numerous past SATs. After reading through the definitions and the examples, I am now able to do sentence completion questions more easily and efficiently. The initial step to bolster the Critical Reading score is to master the sentence completion section, which is impossible without studying vocabulary first. This book will serve as a guide to help students study SAT words effectively.* "

Da-Hyun Rachel Hong (Academies @ Englewood)

Synonym

1. Polarize
    A) Divide
    B) Elicit
    C) Surmise
    D) Deed
    E) Allege

2. Novice
    A) Missive
    B) Seize
    C) Beginner
    D) Absolve
    E) Vanquish

3. Exalt
    A) Neglect
    B) Praise
    C) Preserved
    D) Dispelled
    E) Enshrined

4. Empathy
    A) Vindication
    B) Proposal
    C) Contingencies
    D) Affinity
    E) Reprimand

5. Adversity

A) Dismiss
B) Subvert
C) Argue
D) Retraction
E) Calamity

6. Castigate

A) Deleterious
B) Punish
C) Minuscule
D) Salutary
E) Immediate

7. Capitulate

A) Laud
B) Surrender
C) Resuscitating
D) Flout
E) Relinquish

8. Tedium

A) Prolific
B) Garrulous
C) Abrogate
D) Boredom
E) Patronage

Answer keys

1) A 2) C 3) B 4) D 5) E 6) B 7) B 8) D

Antonym

1. Ruthless
    A) Circumvent
    B) Compassionate
    C) Renounce
    D) Propound
    E) Eschew

2. Espouse
    A) Reject
    B) Adhere
    C) Amorphous
    D) Inedible
    E) Ineffable

3. Nonchalant
    A) Innocuous
    B) Inscrutable
    C) Deny
    D) Awareness
    E) Intense

4. Apathy
    A) Enhance
    B) Reputation
    C) Treachery
    D) Care
    E) Prosperity

5. Unwitting
    A) Downfall
    B) Virtuoso
    C) Intentional
    D) Precocious
    E) Genius

6. Recalcitrant
    A) Fanatical
    B) Obey
    C) Affected
    D) Prodigy
    E) Upstart

7. Imperious
    A) Polite
    B) Modest
    C) Capture
    D) Disrupt
    E) Evoke

8. Fractious
    A) Stir
    B) Evoke
    C) Connotation
    D) Tame
    E) Feeble

9. Paucity
    A) Integrity
    B) Whimsical
    C) Sedulous
    D) Hail
    E) Opulence

Answer keys

1) B 2) A 3) E 4) D 5) C 6) B 7) A 8) D 9) E

1. **Elude** [ih-**lood**]
   verb def: to escape the understanding or perception.
      The answer *eluded* me.

2. **Petrify** [**pe**-truh-fahy]
   verb syn: to benumb; paralyze.
      Michael was *petrified* with fear.

3. **Indefatigable** [in-di-**fat**-i-guh-buhl]
   adj. syn: tireless. (***)
      Many people have made an *indefatigable* effort to improve
      their spoken English proficiencies.

4. **Ominous** [**om**-uh-nuhs]
   adj syn: foretelling; evil. (**)
      Ominous black clouds gathered on the horizon, for a violent storm
      was fast approaching.

5. **Ubiquitous** [yoo-**bik**-wi-tuhs]
   adj def: existing everywhere; omnipresent.
      Ubiquitous little ants in the house drove Jenny crazy.

6. **Virulent** [**vir**-yuh-luhnt]
   adj def: actively poisonous. syn: hostile.
      Laid up with an extremely *virulent* case of measles, he blamed his
      doctors because his recovery took so long. In fact, he became
      quite *virulent* on the subject of the quality of modern medical care.

7. **Benign** [bih-**nahyn**]
   adj syn: kind; favorable. (*)
      Though her *benign* smile and gentle bearing made Miss Goldenberg
      seem a sweet little old lady, in reality she was a tough-minded,
      shrewd observer of human nature.

8. **Inconsequential** [in-kon-si-**kwen**-shul]
adj syn: unimportant; beyond dispute.
> The fact that Harvard University would be too expensive for Lisa without scholarship was *inconsequential*.

9. **Enervate** [**en**-er-veyt]
verb def: to reduce the energy or strength. (***)
> The stress of the operation left her feeling *enervated* feelings of hostility between ranchers and environmentalists.

10. **Corroborate** [kuh-**rob**-uh-reyt]
verb/adj def: supporting with evidence. (*)
> A passerby who had witnessed the crime gave *corroborating* testimony about the presence of the accused person.

11. **Deplore** [dih-**plawr**]
verb def: to feel deep grief.
> The class *deplored* the death of their teacher.

12. **Loquacious** [loh-**kwey**-shuhs]
adj syn: talkative.
> She was naturally *loquacious,* which was a problem in situations in which listening was more important than talking.

13. **Desultory** [**des**-uhl-tawr-ee]
adj syn: at random; rambling.
> Diane had a *desultory* academic record; she had changed majors twelve times in three years.

14. **Phlegmatic** [**fleg**-mat-ik]
adj def: sluggish and unemotional in temperament. (***)
> It was surprising to see Tom, who is normally so *phlegmatic,* acting excitedly.

15. **Peremptory** [puh-**remp**-tuh-ree]
  adj def: leaving no opportunity for denial. (**)
  > The Army General made a *peremptory* command to his subordinators.

16. **Torpid** [**tawr**-pid]
  adj syn: inactive; sluggish. (**)
  > After surgery, the patient was *torpid* until the anesthesia wore off.

17. **Countermand** [**koun**-ter-mand]
  verb syn: to annul; cancel.
  > Protestants were relieved when the Queen *countermanded* her decree that they should be burned at the stake as heretics.

18. **Mercurial** [mer-**kyoor**-ee-uhl]
  adj syn: quick; changeable. (*)
  > Her *mercurial* personality made it difficult to guess how she would react to the bad news.

19. **Concur** [kuhn-**kur**]
  verb syn: to agree in opinion. (**)
  > Justice O'Connor wrote a minority opinion because she did not *concur* with reasoning of her fellow justice.

20. **Maladroit** [mal-uh-**droit**]
  adj syn: clumsy; bungling.
  > Suzy handled a diplomatic crisis in a *maladroit* way.

21. **Harbinger** [**hahr**-bin-jer]
  noun syn: frontier; precursor; forefather. (*)
  > The groundhog's appearance on February 2 is a *harbinger* of spring.

22. **Commodious** [kuh-**moh**-dee-uhs]
  adj syn: roomy; spacious.
  > Rachael was able to stretch out fully in the *commodious* bathtub.

23. Ebb [eb]

noun def: a point of decline.

His fortunes were at low *ebb*.

24. Residue [rez-i-doo]

noun syn: remainder; leftover; remnant.

The fire burned everything, leaving only a *residue* of ash and charred debris.

25. Banal [buh-nal]

adj def: devoid of freshness or quality.

He used *banal* phrase like "Have a nice day" or "Another day, another dollar."

26. Eclectic [ik-klek-tik]

adj syn: selective. (**)

Dr. Newman always follows *eclectic* methods.

27. Continence [kon-tn-uhns]

noun def: self-control; self-restrained.

Lucy exhibited impressive *continence* in steering clear of fattening foods, and she lost 50 pounds.

28. Placate [pley-keyt]

verb syn: to appease; pacify. (*)

The government tried to *placate* an outraged citizenry.

29. Infuriate [in-fyoor-ee-yet]

verb syn: to anger; provoke.

Malcolm knew that his irresponsible behavior would *infuriate* his mother.

30. Euphoria [yoo-fawr-ee-uh]

noun def: agreeableness of sound; pleasing effect the ear. (**)

Euphoria is medically recognized as a mental and emotional state defined as a profound sense of well-being.

31. Choleric [kuh-**ler**-ik]
adj def: extremely irritable or easily angered. (**)
> Kenny showed a *choleric* disposition to his friends.

32. Jocular [**jok**-yuh-ler]
adj syn: joking; jesting; waggish.
> Lisa made a number of *jocular* remarks about opera stars.

33. Demarcation [dee-mahr-**key**-shuhn]
noun def: borderline; act of defining or marking a boundary. (***)
> The Berlin Wall formed a clear *demarcation* between East and West Berlin.

34. Vanity [**van**-i-tee]
noun def: excessive pride in one's appearance.
> Failure to be elected was a great blow to his *vanity*.

35. Ply [plahy]
verb syn: to use diligently; to engage. (**)
> The weaver *plied* the fibers together to make a blanket.

36. Impute [im-**pyoot**]
verb syn: to credit or give responsibility.
> Although Sarah's comments embarrassed me, I don't *impute* any ill to her.

37. Emulate [**em**-yuh-leyt]
verb syn: to equal; excel.
> Lynn *emulated* Evo as a concert pianist.

38. Strident [**strahyd**-nt]
adj syn: grating; creaking. (**)
> Jason was unable to sleep last night due to the *strident* insects flying in his room.

39. Discomfit [dis-**kuhm**-fit]
verb syn: to frustrate.

Discomfited by the interviewer's unexpected question, Peter could only stammer in reply.

40. Connoisseur [kon-uh-sur]
noun def: a person who is especially competent to pass critical judgment. (*)

Lim is traditionally a *connoisseur* of modern art.

41. Subtle [**suht**-l]
adj syn: fine; delicate.

It is difficult for ordinary people to perceive *subtle* irony.

42. Hindsight [**hahynd**-sahyt]
noun def: perception of events after they happen. (**)

In *hindsight*, Hank realized that drinking the entire bottle of vodka himself was probably not a wise idea.

43. Premonition [pree-**muh**-nish-uhm]
noun def: a feeling of anticipation of or anxiety over a future event.

He had a vague *premonition* of danger.

44. Antagonism [an-**tag**-uh-niz-uhm]
noun syn: an opposing force; principle.

Her plan to become an actress met with the *antagonism* of her family.

45. Eternal [ih-**tur**-nl]
adj syn: ceaseless; endless. (**)

In modern society not many people believe in *eternal* love.

Synonym

1. Subtle
- A) Integrity
- B) Sophisticated
- C) Levity
- D) Prediction
- E) Empathy

2. Emulate
- A) Copy
- B) Endorsed
- C) Neglected
- D) Detested
- E) Ornithology

3. Demarcation
- A) Topography
- B) Optimistic
- C) Boundary
- D) Mercurial
- E) Alchemy

4. Continence
- A) Magnanimous
- B) Taciturn
- C) Docile
- D) Abstinence
- E) Morbid

5. Banal
    A) Cathartic
    B) Pedantic
    C) Flippant
    D) Reticent
    E) Hackneyed

6. Mercurial
    A) Specificity
    B) Changeable
    C) Loftiness
    D) Profundity
    E) Inclusiveness

7. Peremptory
    A) Imperative
    B) Alacrity
    C) Querulous
    D) Languor
    E) Disaffected

8. Elude
    A) Remission
    B) Fortify
    C) Retrieve
    D) Escape
    E) Scourge

Answer keys

1) B 2) A 3) C 4) D 5) E 6) B 7) A 8) D

Antonym

1. Antagonism
    A) Harmony
    B) Resentment
    C) Diplomatic
    D) Decorum
    E) Diffident

2. Concur
    A) Aplomb
    B) Crucial
    C) Disagree
    D) Renunciation
    E) Indispensable

3. Choleric
    A) Dissemination
    B) Detrimental
    C) Tangential
    D) Calm
    E) Relevant

4. Infuriate
    A) Benevolent
    B) Introspective
    C) Belligerent
    D) Complacent
    E) Please

5. Maladroit
    A) Insistent
    B) Skillful
    C) Melodious
    D) Inaudible
    E) Strident

6. Ebb
    A) Discontinuance
    B) Increase
    C) Waiver
    D) Census
    E) Levy

7. Loquacious
    A) Taciturn
    B) Chronicles
    C) Averts
    D) Surmise
    E) Libertine

8. Virulent
    A) Impetuous
    B) Obstinate
    C) Harmless
    D) Concord
    E) Ubiquitous

9. Enervate
    A) Solicit
    B) Contrite
    C) Transitory
    D) Energize
    E) Occlude

Answer keys

1) A 2) C 3) D 4) E 5) B 6) B 7) A 8) C 9) D

1. **Carnivorous** [khar-**niv**-er-uhs]
   adj syn: flesh-eating.
   > The lion is a *carnivorous* animal.

2. **Obdurate** [**ob**-doo-rit]
   adj syn: unwilling to change; stubborn.
   > Despite the many pleas he received, the governor was *obdurate* in his refusal to grant clemency to the convicted murderer.

3. **Implicit** [im-**plis**-it]
   adj syn: implied, not directly expressed. (**)
   > In her writings the author showed a sense of moral duty *implicit*.

4. **Frivolity** [fri-**vol**-i-tee]
   noun def: the quality or state of being frivolous.
   > It was a *frivolity* he had a hard time living down.

5. **Vignette** [vin-**yet**]
   noun syn: decorative design.
   > The writer's clever little *vignette* was published in a respected literary magazine.

6. **Nimble** [**nim**-buhl]
   adj def: quick and light in movement. (***)
   > Jack has just finished reading a story with a *nimble* plot.

7. **Digression** [dih-**gresh**-uhn]
   noun def: wondering away from the subject. (**)
   > Nobody minded when Professor Renoir's lectures wandered away from their official themes; his *digressions* were always more fascinating than the topic of the day.

8. **Robust** [roh-**buhst**]
   adj syn: vigorous; strong. (*)
   > After pumping iron and taking karate for six months, Steve has become a *robust* man.

9. **Appropriate** [uh-**proh**-pree-it]
   verb def: to take without permission. (**)
   He *appropriated* the trust fund for himself.

10. **Vigilance** [**vij**-uh-luhns]
    noun def: state or quality of being watchfulness.
    Vigilance is required in the event of treachery.

11. **Embezzle** [em-**bez**-uhl]
    verb def: to steal money or property; forfeit. (***)
    The church treasurer was found to have *embezzled* thousands of
    dollars by writing phony checks on the church bank account.

12. **Sequester** [se-**kwes**-ter]
    verb syn: to remove; to set apart.
    The witness in the mafia case was *sequestered* for his own
    protection when it was determined that his life might be in danger.

13. **Judicious** [joo-**dish**-uhs]
    adj syn: wise; sensible; well advised.
    Tim has finally completed a *judicious* selection of document.

14. **Obnoxious** [uhb-**nok**-shuhs]
    adj syn: harmful; odious.
    John's *obnoxious* behavior in class made his teacher upset.

15. **Equivocate** [ih-kwiv-uh-**keyt**]
    verb syn: ambiguous; opaque. (**)
    When asked directly for his position on disarmament, the
    candidate only *equivocated*.

16. **Ambivalent** [am-**biv**-uh-luhns]
    adj syn: uncertainty; fluctuation.
    Jenny seemed to make an *ambivalent* attitude towards the issue
    she was facing.

17. Novelty [nov-uh-l-tee]
noun def: a novel or new occurrence, experience, or proceeding. (*)
His sarcastic witticisms had ceased being an entertaining *novelty*.

18. Inarticulate [in-ahr-tik-yuh-lit]
adj def: not fully expressed.
A voice choked with *inarticulate* agony.

19. Remiss [ri-mis]
adj syn: negligent; lazy. (**)
Harrison is terribly *remiss* in his work.

20. Lithe [lahyth]
adj syn: bending readily; pliant; flexible. (*)
Yoga requires a *lithe* body.

21. Despondent [dih-spun-duhnt]
noun def: feeling or showing profound hopelessness.
He turned out to be *despondent* about failing health.

22. Submissive [suhb-mis-iv]
adj def: tending to be meek and submit. (***)
The *submissive* wolf cringed at the feet of the alpha male, leader of the pack.

23. Rectitude [rek-ti-tood]
noun def: rightness of principle or conduct. (**)
Young women used to be shipped off to fishing schools to teach them proper manners and *rectitude*.

24. Dearth [durth]
noun syn: inadequate supply.
There is a *dearth* of good engineers.

25. Surfeit [**sur**-fit]

noun syn: excess; an excessive amount. (**)

Because of the *surfeit* of pigs, pork prices have never been lower.

26. Contrive [kuhn-**trahyv**]

verb syn: to bring about; scheme.

McArthur *contrived* a meeting with the president.

27. Decrepit [dih-**krep**-it]

adj syn: weakened by old age; feeble.

A *decrepit* man can hardly walk.

28. Spurious [**spyoor**-ee-uhs]

adj syn: lacking authenticity; counterfeit. (***)

Quoting from a *spurious* bible, the cult leader declared that all property should be assigned over to him.

29. Strut [struht]

noun def: pompous walk.

Blimp's *strut* as he marched about the parade ground revealed him for what he was: a pompous buffoon.

30. Squalid [**skwol**-id]

adj syn: filthy; morally repulsive. (***)

The *squalid* living conditions in the tenement building outraged the new tenets.

31. Duplicity [doo-**pli**-i-tee]

noun syn: deception. (**)

Diplomatic relations between the two superpowers were outwardly friendly, yet characterized by *duplicity*.

32. Disapprove [dis-**proov**]

verb def: to prove to be false. (***)

Peter *disapproved* Brian's claim.

33. Affectionate [uh-**fek**-shuh-nit]
adj syn: love; tender. (*)
> Kenny has four *affectionate* brothers.

34. Obtuse [uhb-**toos**]
adj syn: dull; not quick.
> What can you do with somebody who is so *obtuse* that he cannot even tell that you are insulting him?

35. Devoid [dih-**void**]
verb syn: deplete; strip.
> Imprisonment *devoids* a person of humanity.

36. Commemorate [kuh-**mem**-uh-reyt]
verb def: to serve as a memorial.
> The monument *commemorates* the signing of the Declaration of Independence.

37. Replicate [**rep**-li-kit]
verb syn: duplicate; copy.
> If you are going to *replicate* last year's profit of margins, we are going to have to work really hard.

38. Remuneration [ri-myoo-nuh-**rey**-shuhn]
noun def: something that reward; pay. (**)
> He received little *remuneration* for his services.

39. Perquisite [**pur**-kwuh-zit]
noun syn: benefit; privilege.
> Among the president's *perquisites* were free use of a company car and paid membership in a country club.

40. Venal [**veen**-l]
adj def: characterized by bribery. (***)
> Tom and Jim made a *venal* agreement.

41. Gratification [grat-uh-fi-**key**-shuhn]
noun syn: free; voluntary.

    Matt's snubbing of his old friend seemed *gratification* as there had been no bad blood between the two of them previously.

42. Provisional [pruh-**vizh**-uh-nl]
adj syn: tentative. (**)

    Edward's appointment was *provisional*; he needed the approval of the board of directors before it would be made permanent.

43. Fallow [fal-oh]
adj def: not in use.

    My creative energies have lain *fallow* this year.

44. Frenetic [fruh-**net**-ik]
adj def: widely frantic. (**)

    The *frenetic* manager worked insane hours, trying desperately to finish the important project on time.

45. Chimerical [ki-**mer**-i-kuhl]
adj. syn: unreal; imaginary.

    The inventor's plan seemed *chimerical* to the conservative businessman from whom he was asking for financial support.

“ *Great book! This book will definitely help you to prepare for the SAT. The arduous words and the little mini-quizzes at the end will help! It is a must-buy book!* **”**

Juliana Lee *(Palisades Park Junior-Senior High School)*

Synonym

1. Fallow
A) Provincial
B) Not used
C) Zealot
D) Partisan
E) Indulgent

2. Remuneration
A) Compensate
B) Maverick
C) Altruistic
D) Rebel
E) Vicarious

3. Disapprove
A) Innovative
B) Dissuade
C) Criticize
D) Dissuade
E) Exotic

4. Spurious
A) Alienate
B) Intensive
C) Entice
D) Fake
E) Ominous

5. Surfeit
    A) Tantalize
    B) Fading
    C) Symptom
    D) Novelty
    E) Excess

6. Remiss
    A) Diversity
    B) Myriad
    C) Careless
    D) Starkness
    E) Vibrant

7. Vigilance
    A) Watch
    B) Toxicity
    C) Varying
    D) Hail
    E) Ostracize

8. Obdurate
    A) Parochial
    B) Intrepid
    C) Copious
    D) Stubborn
    E) Florid

Answer keys

1) B 2) A 3) C 4) D 5) E 6) C 7) A 8) D

Antonym

1. Provisional
> A) Eradicated
> B) Permanent
> C) Accosted
> D) Undermine
> E) Underscore

2. Devoid
> A) Lauded
> B) Superseded
> C) Reprove
> D) Sufficient
> E) Expedited

3. Squalid
> A) Articulate
> B) Immature
> C) Clean
> D) Disturb
> E) Callow

4. Decrepit
> A) Skeptic
> B) Pundit
> C) Dilettante
> D) Insurgent
> E) Healthy

5. Submissive
> A) Dominance
> B) Edible
> C) Longevity
> D) Unpalatable
> E) Disobey

6. Obnoxious
    A) Harmful
    B) Agreeable
    C) Mortality
    D) Subterfuge
    E) Suppress

7. Nimble
    A) Slow
    B) Agility
    C) Coercion
    D) Innuendo
    E) Synthesize

8. Sequester
    A) Surpass
    B) Preamble
    C) Integrate
    D) Aspersion
    E) Grudge

9. Ambivalent
    A) Reverent
    B) Vapid
    C) Regime
    D) Certain
    E) Meddlesome

Answer keys

1) B 2) D 3) C 4) E 5) E 6) B 7) A 8) C 9) D

1. **Perfunctory** [per-**fuhngk**-tuh-ree]
   adj def: lacking interest. (*)
   > In his lectures he reveals himself to be merely a *perfunctory* speaker.

2. **Sedentary** [**sed**-n-ter-ee]
   adj def: requiring much sitting.
   > When Officer Samson was given a desk job, she had trouble getting used to *sedentary* work after years on the street.

3. **Truculent** [**truhk**-yuh-luhnt]
   adj syn: fierce; cruel; brutal. (*)
   > Dr. Nash made a *truculent* criticism to the Jean's research paper.

4. **Pugnacious** [puhg-**ney**-shuhs]
   adj def: inclined quarrel or fight readily. (*)
   > The serene eighty-year-old used to be a *pugnacious* troublemaker in her youth, but she is softer now.

5. **Underscore** [**uhn**-der-skawr]
   verb syn: to stress; emphasize. (**)
   > The recent tragedy *underscores* the danger of disregarding safety rules.

6. **Sequel** [see-*kwuhl*]
   noun def: anything that follows. (**)
   > I hear that they are making another *sequel* to the Friday the 13th movies.

7. **Underestimate** [uhn-der-**es**-tuh-meyt]
   verb def: to estimate at too low a value.
   > Many SAT test takers seemed to *underestimate* their potential academic abilities to improve their test scores.

8. **Purport** [per-**pawrt**]
   noun syn: to present; profess; calm. (**)
   > Tommy did not read the letter aloud, but all present were informed of its *purport*.

9. Delectable [dih-**lek**-tuh-buhl]
noun syn: appetizing food or dish.

A buffet table was spread with *delectable*.

10. Pique [peek]
noun def: fleeting feeling of hurt pride. (*)

In a fit of *pique*, the writer tossed his manuscript into the fire after his friend criticize it.

11. Savory [**sey**-vuh-ree]
noun def: pleasant or agreeable in taste or smell.

He really enjoyed a *savory* aroma emitting from a bunch of flowers.

12. Recapitulate [ree-kuh-**pich**-uh-leyt]
verb def: to review by a brief summary. (**)

After the long-winded president had finished his speech, his assistant *recapitulated* the points he had made for the press.

13. Cogent [**koh**-juhnt]
adj syn: convincing; incisive presentation.

Paul got promoted by providing a *cogent* presentation about the project his company was about to invest a huge amount of money in.

14. Dissipate [**dis**-uh-peyt]
verb syn: to scatter; disperse.

The sun shone and the mist *dissipated*.

15. Desiccate [**des**-i-keyt]
verb syn: to dry thoroughly; to dry up. (*)

After a few weeks of lying on the desert's baking sands, the cow's carcass became completely *desiccated*

16. Curmudgeon [ker-**muhj**-uhn]
noun syn: malcontent; stingy; miser. (***)

The old man was a notorious *curmudgeon* who yelled at anyone who disturbed him for any reason.

17. Penitent [pen-i-tuhnt]
adj def: expressing sorrow for sins.
The victim's family claimed that the murderer did not feel *penitent* and therefore should not have been released from prison.

18. Tightwad [tahyt-wod]
noun def: a close-fisted or stingy person
Her husband is such a *tightwad* that he never wants to go out to dinner.

19. Felicitous [fil-lis-i-tuhs]
adj syn: suitable; appropriate. (***)
The father of bride made a *felicitous* speech at the wedding, contributing to the success of the event.

20. Austere [aw-steer]
adj def: rigorous self-discipline and severely moral.
Josh found himself being unable to put up with the *austere* quality of life in the convent.

21. Tantamount [tan-tuh-mount]
adj def: equivalent in value or significance. (*)
Her refusal to defend herself against the accusation was *tantamount* to a confession in the eyes of the police officers.

22. Betrothed [bi-trohthd]
verb def: to arrange for the marriage.
The couple was *betrothed* with the approval of both families.

23. Heuristic [hyoo-ris-tik]
adj def: encouraging a person to learn.
Many teachers have recently implemented *heuristic* teaching methods in their class.

24. Upheaval [uhp-**hee**-vuhl]
noun def: strong or violent change. syn: disturbance. (***)
The Second World War got people in the world into
the *upheaval* environment.

25. Convoke [kuhn-**vohk**]
verb syn: to call together.
The principal of the local high school immediately *convoked*
teachers to deal with a student's misconduct in class.

26. Totter [**tot**-er]
verb def: to walk or go with faltering steps
A child *tottered* across the room.

27. Defoliate [dee-**foh**-lee-yet]
verb def: to destroy or cause widespread loss of leaves.
The government decided to *defoliate* an area of forest by using
chemical sprays.

28. Disavow [dis-uh-**vou**]
verb def: to disclaim knowledge of.
Scott *disavowed* the remark that had been attributed to them.

29. Jettison [**jet**-uh-suhn]
verb syn: discard; throw away; eject. (**)
The captain was forced to decide to *jettison* many necessary things
in order not to let his ship sink deep into the sea. .

30. Circumlocution [sur-kuhm-loh-**kyoo**-shuhn]
noun def: a roundabout expression. (*)
Mr. Park avoided discussing the real issues with
endless *circumlocution*.

31. Contemplate [kon-tuhm-**pleyt**]
verb syn: to think fully or over. (***)
Jane always *contemplates* buying something valuable.

32. Thespian [thes-pee-uh n]
adj def: pertaining to tragedy or climatic art in general

Although she's "acted" in a couple of horror movies, I'd hardly call her one of our more promising *thespians*.

33. Phlegmatic [fleg-mat-ik]
adj def: sluggish or unemotional in temperament. (***)

It was surprising to see Tim, who is normally so *phlegmatic*, acting excited.

34. Eulogy [yoo-luh-jee]
noun syn: to praise highly. (**)

Brian's best friend gave the *eulogy*, outlining his many achievements and talents.

35. Jeopardize [jep-er-dahyz]
verb def: to put in danger.

Terrorist attacks *jeopardize* the fragile peace in the Middle East.

36. Pilfer [pil-fer]
verb syn: to steal. (*)

Tom has an abnormal habit of *pilfering* money from his friend, even though he is known as a multi-millionaire.

37. Pontificate [pon-tif-i-kit]
verb def: to speak in a pompous or dogmatic. (**)

Did he *pontificate* about the responsibilities of a good citizen?

38. Dispel [dih-spel]
verb syn: to drive away; to scatter.

The bright sunlight eventually *dispelled* the morning mist.

39. Virtuoso [vur-choo-oh-soh]
noun def: highly skilled artist. syn: maestro.

The child prodigy Monet grew into a *virtuoso* whose violin performances thrilled millions.

40. Scathing [skey-thing]

adj def: harshly critical. (***)

After the *scathing* criticism her book of poems received, Alicia swore off poetry writing for good.

41. Belie [bih-lahy]

verb def: to show to be false.

His trembling hands *belied* his claim voice.

42. Propagate [proh-uh-geyt]

verb def: to increase in extent. syn: to breed; produce; engender.

The crack will *propagate* only to this joint.

43. Perfidious [per-fid-ee-iuhs]

adj syn: disloyal. (*)

The actress's *perfidious* companion revealed all of her intimate secrets to the gossip columnist.

44. Veracity [vuh-ras-i-tee]

noun def: habitual observance of truth in speech. (**)

John was not noted for his *veracity*.

45. Zealot [zel-uht]

noun syn: fanatic.

Though Glenn was devout, he was no *zealot*; he never tried to force his beliefs on his friends.

Synonym

1. Scathing
- A) Cajolery
- B) Undertake
- C) Severe
- D) Chicanery
- E) Precedent

2. Pilfer
- A) Steal
- B) Altruistic
- C) Placatory
- D) Benign
- E) Fortuitous

3. Eulogize
- A) Punctilious
- B) Praise
- C) Pioneer
- D) Mimic
- E) Progenitor

4. Contemplation
- A) Exploit
- B) Devotee
- C) Jettison
- D) Consideration
- E) Forebear

5. Underscore

A) Negligible
B) Migration
C) Vital
D) Combine
E) Stress

6. Upheaval

A) Integral
B) Inexplicable
C) Proximity
D) Eradication
E) Disturbance

7. Curmudgeon

A) Miser
B) Paragon
C) Opulence
D) Dilettante
E) Oblivion

8. Truculent

A) Stilted
B) Havoc
C) Brutal
D) Whimsical
E) Grasp

Answer keys

1) C 2) A 3) B 4) D 5) E 6) E 7) A 8) C

Antonym

1. Perfidious
>   A) Loyal
>   B) Prodigy
>   C) Anonymity
>   D) Guru
>   E) Seclusion

2. Belie
>   A) Charlatan
>   B) Enigmatic
>   C) Honest
>   D) Abrasive
>   E) Impromptu

3. Dispel
>   A) Meticulous
>   B) Lackluster
>   C) Ungainly
>   D) Gather
>   E) Autocratic

4. Phlegmatic
>   A) Unflappable
>   B) Passionate
>   C) Egotistical
>   D) Demonstrative

5. Disavow
>   A) Rancor
>   B) Lethargy
>   C) Commiseration
>   D) Compunction
>   E) Agree

6. Austere
    A) Unerring
    B) Meek
    C) Dexterous
    D) Circumspect
    E) Dehydrate

7. Mitigate
    A) Dissolute
    B) Feverish
    C) Aggravate
    D) Resilient
    E) Debilitated

8. Veracity
    A) Ominous
    B) Virulent
    C) Gallop
    D) False
    E) Impede

9. Dissipate
    A) Lethargic
    B) Irascible
    C) Scatter
    D) Flatter
    E) Gather

Answer keys

1) A 2) C 3) D 4) B 5) E 6) B 7) C 8) D 9) E

1. **Autonomy** [aw-**ton**-uh-mee]
   noun def: self-government.
   > The rebels demanded *autonomy* from Spain.

2. **Embellish** [em-**bel**-ish]
   verb syn: to decorate. (**)
   > Lisa always *embellished* her room with a variety of flowers.

3. **Emollient** [ih-**mol**-yuhnt]
   adj syn: to soften; relax.
   > Astra applied *emollient* lotions for her face.

4. **Perdition** [per-**dish**-uhn]
   noun def: complete and utter loss.
   > Faust brought *perdition* upon himself when he made a deal with the Devil in exchange for power.

5. **Anesthetic** [an-uhs-**thet**-ik]
   adj def: physically insensitive.
   > Halothane is used to produce an *anesthetic* state.

6. **Inoculate** [ih-**nok**-yuh-leyt]
   verb def: to prevent a disease. (*)
   > Pasteur found that he could prevent rabies by *inoculating* patients with the virus that causes the disease.

7. **Verbatim** [ver-**bey**-tim]
   adj def: skilled at recording or noting down.
   > Jessica has been known as a *verbatim* stenographer.

8. **Cursory** [**kur**-suh-ree]
   adj def: going rapidly over something. (***)
   > He made a *cursory* glance at a newspaper article.

9. **Squalor** [**skwol**-er]
   adj syn: filth; misery.
   > Chris lives in a *squalor* house.

10. Proximity [prok-**sim**-tee]

noun def: nearness in place, order. (**)

Tim was careful to put the glass out of reach, since the toddler loved to yank down objects in her *proximity*.

11. Adumbrate [a-**duhm**-breyt]

verb syn: to sketch; outline.

There was only time to *adumbrate* an escape plan before the cyclone hit.

12. Mellifluous [muh-**lif**-loo-uhs]

adj syn: sweetly; smoothly. (**)

Esther appeared to have a *mellifluous* voice.

13. Secant [**see**-kant]

noun def: straight line interesting a curve at two points.

The mathematician used the *secant* to calculate the area of the curved shape.

14. Caucus [**kaw**-kuhs]

verb def: to bring up for discussion in a caucus.

The group *caucused* the meeting.

15. Prognosticate [prog-**nos**-ti-keyt]

verb syn: to assume; conjecture.

Birds *prognosticate* spring.

16. Seamy [**see**-mee]

adj def: unpleasant or sordid; low

The newspaper revealed that Ms. Eisenstein was deeply involved in a *seamy* corruption scandal.

17. Forthright [**fawrth**-rahyt]

adj syn: direct; outspoken. (*)

It is sometimes difficult to be *forthright* and not give offense.

18. **Coerce** [**koh**-urs]
    verb def: to compel by force.
    They *coerced* him into signing the document.

19. **Obsolete** [ob-suh-**leet**]
    adj def: no longer in general use. (***)
    Many things are becoming *obsolete*.

20. **Satiate** [**sey**-shee-yet]
    verb syn: to satisfy. (**)
    His desire for power was so great that nothing less than
    complete control of the country could *satiate* it.

21. **Berate** [bih-**reyt**]
    verb syn: scold; rebuke.
    He *berated* his best friend in public.

22. **Plummet** [**pluhm**-it]
    verb syn: to fall; plunge. (**)
    Marvin screamed as he watched his new Ferrari *plummet* into
    the depth of the ravine.

23. **Curtail** [ker-**teyl**]
    verb syn: to shorten; brief. (***)
    Because of the military emergence, all soldiers on leave were
    ordered to *curtail* their absences and return to duty.

24. **Prosaic** [proh-**zey**-ik]
    adj syn: dull; commonplace.
    Simon's *prosaic* style bored his writing teacher to tears, and
    she dreaded having to mark his essays.

25. **Censorious** [sen-**sawr**-ee-uhs]
    adj syn: severely critical.
    Saddam, unconcerned by the *censorious* attitude of the U.N.,
    continued his nuclear weapons testing.

26. Morose [muh-rohs]

adj syn: gloomy; sullen.

After Chuck's girlfriend dumped him, he lay around the house for a couple of days, feeling *morose*.

27. Tedium [tee-dee-uhm]

noun def: long and tiresome. (**)

For the most people, watching the Weather Channel for 24 hours would be sheer *tedium*.

28. Laggard [lag-erd]

noun def: in a manner of laggard. syn: casually; unhurriedly. (***)

He behaved in a manner of *laggard*.

29. Refectory [ri-fek-tuh-ree]

noun def: room where meals are served. syn: ballroom; chamber.

The students rushed down to the *refectory* for their evening meal.

30. Compendious [kuhm-pen-dee-uhs]

adj def: in a brief form; concise. syn: condensed; abbreviated.

Dr. Pinker wrote a *compendious* history of the world.

31. Grandiloquence [gran-dil-uh-kwuhns]

noun syn: pompous talk; fancy. (**)

The pompous headmistress was notorious for her *grandiloquence* as well as for her ostentatious clothes.

32. Malleable [mal-ee-uh-buhl]

adj def: able to be changed, shaped. syn: flexible; compatible.

Gold is a very useful metal because it is so *malleable*.

33. Whimsical [hwim-zi-kuhl]

adj syn: capricious; changeable. (****)

Her writing showed *whimsical* notions of human behavior.

34. Disdain [dis-**deyn**]

verb def: regard with scorn. syn: antipathy; aversion.

The gorgeous contestant *disdained* her competitors, certain that she would win the Miss America crown.

35. Diconcert [dis-kuhn-**surt**]

verb syn: to confuse; embarrass. (***)

When the hallway bells began to ring halfway through her lecture, the speaker was *disconcerted* and didn't know what to do.

36. Glower [**glou**-er]

verb syn: to glare; to stare angrily.

The cranky waitress *glowered* at the indecisive customer.

37. Coalesce [koh-uh-**les**]

verb syn: to unite. (**)

The various groups *coalesced* into a crowd.

38. Intersperse [in-ter-**spurs**]

verb syn: to mix; to combine.

Mushrooms were *interspersed* among the bushes and clumps of moss in the shady forest.

39. Penchant [**pen**-chuhnt]

noun syn: strong inclination. syn: affection; affinity; disposition.

He had a strong *penchant* for outdoor sports.

40. Denigrate [**den**-i-greyt]

verb syn: to criticize; belittle. (***)

The firm's new president tried to explain his plans for improving the company without seeming to *denigrate* the work of his predecessor.

41. Detractor   [dih-**trakt**-er]

noun def: someone who belittles or disparages. syn: censor;
critic; defamer. (**)
The singer has many *detractors* who consider his music boring,
inane, and sentimental.

42. Censure   [**sen**-sher]

noun syn: disapproval; criticism. (***)
The newspapers were unanimous in their *censure* of the
tax proposal.

43. Accolade   [**ak**-uh-leyd]

noun syn: praise; distinction.
The protagonist of the movie received *accolades* from the press.

44. Enthrall   [en-**thrawl**]

verb syn: to enchant; charm.
When the Swedish singer Jenny Lind toured America in the
nineteenth century, her beauty and talent *enthralled* audiences.

45. Accrue   [uh-**kroo**]

verb syn: to accumulate; to grow by addition.
Before he knew it, Cliff had *accrued* an overwhelmingly large debt.

" *This book is really helpful for me in memorizing the SAT
words, as I discovered when I took the real SAT tests. I am so
confident that this book will improve my Critical Reading score
even more next time.* **"**

Hanna K *(Queen of Peace High School)*

Synonym

1. Inoculate
- A) Disheartened
- B) Immunize
- C) Ornate
- D) Elaborate
- E) Spartan

2. Mellifluous
- A) Vivid
- B) Aphorism
- C) Mellow
- D) Epistles
- E) Penchant

3. Obsolete
- A) Anachronistic
- B) Locution
- C) Yen
- D) Paradigm
- E) Antipathy

4. Berate
- A) Intimate
- B) Criticize
- C) Literal
- D) Objective
- E) Secretive

5. Morose
    A) Incompetent
    B) Contentious
    C) Expansive
    D) Abstruse
    E) Gloomy

6. Laggardly
    A) Fraudulent
    B) Tacit
    C) Slow
    D) Acute
    E) Sonorous

7. Malleable
    A) Ubiquitous
    B) Mitigate
    C) Latent
    D) Exacerbate
    E) Pliable

8. Emollient
    A) Relax
    B) Detach
    C) Perplex
    D) Devoid
    E) Outstrip

Answer keys

1) B   2) C   3) A   4) B   5) E   6) C   7) E   8) A

Antonym

1. Cursory
    A) Meticulous
    B) Negligent
    C) Alleviate
    D) Ephemeral
    E) Palliate

2. Squalor
    A) Pervasive
    B) Enhance
    C) Clean
    D) Appease
    E) Deprecate

3. Ineffable
    A) Enlighten
    B) Describable
    C) Initiate
    D) Bolster
    E) Gloated

4. Satiate
    A) Despaired
    B) Misbehavior
    C) Dominant
    D) Dissatisfy
    E) Irrelevant

5. Curtail
    A) Proximity
    B) Precise
    C) Persuasive
    D) Extend
    E) Vague

6. Tedium
    A) Boredom
    B) Analyze
    C) Illuminate
    D) Plagiarize
    E) Interest

7. Whimsical
    A) Reasonable
    B) Contradict
    C) Magnitude
    D) Preservation
    E) Vulnerability

8. Verbatim
    A) Abhor
    B) Spurious
    C) Inaccurately
    D) Pliant
    E) Clumsy

9. Coerce
    A) Fraction
    B) Stalk
    C) Stoic
    D) Convince
    E) Artificial

Answer keys

1) A 2) C 3) B 4) D 5) D 6) E 7) A 8) C 9) D

1. **Foible** [foi-buhl]
   noun syn: minor; weakness; character flaw. (*)
   > Her habit of licking out the centers of Oreo cookies is a *foible*, not a serious character flaw.

2. **Filibuster** [fil-uh-buhs-ter]
   noun verb def: use of obstructive tactics in a legislative assembly to prevent adoption of a measure.
   > Democrats *filibustered* for hours, desperately trying to prevent the adoption of the Republican measure.

3. **Foliate** [foh-lee-it]
   adj verb syn: developing; flourishing. (**)
   > The plant looked dead, so Victor was astonished when it began to *foliate*.

4. **Prepossessing** [pree-puh-zes-ing]
   adj syn: attractive; engaging; appealing.
   > The young man's *prepossessing* appearance and manner made him the most eligible bachelor at the party.

5. **Swindle** [swin-dl]
   noun syn: to cheat; deceive. (***)
   > Identity theft has become one of the most frequent and feared *swindles* of our time.

6. **Tepid** [tep-id]
   adj syn: lukewarm; apathetic. (*)
   > In geography, *tepid* latitudes of the globe lie between the tropics and polar circles.

7. **Convex** [kon-veks]
   adj def: curved outward; arched; bent
   > The *convex* shape of his potbelly contrasted sharply with his wife's tautly concave stomach.

8. **Mercurial** [mer-**kyoor**-ee-uhl]

   adj syn: capricious; changing; fickle. (**)

   > Quick as quicksilver to change, he was *mercurial* in nature.

9. **Arbiter** [**ahr**-bi-ter]

   noun def: a person empowered to decide matters at issue; judge.

   > Since the couple could not come to agreement, a judge was forced to play an *arbiter* for their divorce proceedings.

10. **Fetter** [**fet**-er]

    noun syn: chain; shackle.

    > Boredom puts *fetters* upon the imagination.

11. **Forgo** [fawr-**goh**]

    verb syn: to stop; prevent; restrain. (***)

    > In an effort to lose weight, Lisa decided to *forgo* dessert for the next month or so.

12. **Flamboyant** [flam-**boi**-uhnt]

    adj syn: florid; ornate.

    > The president made a *flamboyant* speech about a policy of secondary school education.

13. **Fraternize** [**frat**-er-nahyz]

    verb def: to associate with on friendly terms; keep company with.

    > Although baseball player aren't supposed to *fraternize* with their opponents, players from opposing teams often chat before games.

14. **Circumference** [ser-**kuhm**-fer-uhns]

    noun syn: boundary; circle. (**)

    > The space shuttle set a course around the *circumference* of the Earth.

15. **Circuitous** [ser-**kyoo**-i-tuhs]

    adj syn: roundabout.

    > The cab driver took a *circuitous* route to the airport, making me miss my plane.

16. Stymie [stahy-mee]
verb syn: hinder; block; thwart.
> The police effort to capture the bank robber was *stymied* when he escaped through a rear window.

17. Subliminal [suhb-lim-uh-nl]
adj syn: subconscious; imperceptible.
> *Subliminal* message flash by so quickly on the TV screen that viewers are not consciously aware that they have seen them.

18. Civility [si-vil-i-tee]
noun syn: courtesy; politeness. (**)
> The subway ticket seller treated his customers with the utmost *civility,* which they appreciated.

19. Deviate [dee-vee-yet]
verb syn: stray; wander.
> As long as you don't *deviate* from the trail, you should be fine out there in the wilderness.

20. Sumptuous [suhmp-choo-uhs]
adj syn: lavish; splendid. (**)
> The banquet was a *sumptuous* affair, including a seven-course meal and quarts of champagne.

21. Superannuated [soo-pur-an-yoo-yet]
adj syn: too old; obsolete; outdated.
> The manual typewriter has become *superannuated,* although a few loyal diehards still swear by it.

22. Domineer [dom-uh-neer]
verb syn: to rule over. (*)
> The castle *domineers* the town.

23. Dissension [dis-sen-shuhn]
noun verb def: to disagree with the methods. (***)
Two of the justices *dissented* from the majority decision.

24. Instigate [in-sti-geyt]
verb syn: to urge; provoke.
A demagogue tried to *instigate* the people to revolt.

25. Stratify [strat-uh-fay]
verb def: to arrange into layers.
Many Indians use the concept of caste to *stratify* society into levels ranging from the "Untouchables" to the Brahmins.

26. Promulgate [prom-uhl-geyt]
verb syn: to declare.
Lincoln signed the Proclamation that freed the slaves in 1862, but he waited several months to *promulgate* it.

27. Secrete [si-kreet]
verb syn: to discharge. (**)
Glands in the mouth *secrete* saliva, a liquid that helps in digestion.

28. Reclusive [rek-loo-siv]
adj def: withdrawn from society. (***)
During the last years of her life, actress Greta Garbo led a *reclusive* existence, rarely appearing in public.

29. Recuperate [ri-koo-puh-reyt]
verb syn: to regain health.
Although she left hospital days after her operation, it took her a few weeks to fully *recuperate*.

30. Simian [sim-ee-uhn]
adj syn: to apelike.
Early man was more *simian* in appearance than modern man, as he was more closely related to apes.

31. Cerebral [suh-**ree**-bruhl]
adj def: betraying or characterized by the use of the intellect rather than intuition. (**)
> A young man has given more to *cerebral* pursuits than to sporting activities.

32. Pathology [puh-**thol**-uh-jee]
noun def: the study of disease.
> Some people believe that high rates of crime are symptoms of an underlying social *pathology*.

33. Perfunctory [per-**fuhngk**-tuh-ree]
adj syn: routine. (**)
> In his lecture, Dr. Schmidt reveals himself to be a merely *perfunctory* speaker.

34. Deface [dih-**feys**]
verb def: mar the surface or appearance. (***)
> He *defaced* a wall by writing on it.

35. Atrocious [uh-**troh**-shuhs]
adj syn: monstrous; shockingly bad; wicked.
> The British officer committed the *atrocious* act of slaughtering a large group of peaceful Indian villagers.

36. Bereft [bih-**reft**]
adj syn: lacking or deprived of something. (***)
> A cheap motel completely *bereft of all amenities*

37. Tenuous [**ten**-yoo-uhs]
adj syn: slight importance. (**)
> He holds a rather *tenuous* position in history.

38. Grovel [**gruhv**-uhl]
verb syn: to humble oneself.
> The dog *groveled* at his owner's feet, hoping for a few table scraps.

39. Interlope [in-ter-lohp]
noun verb syn: trespasser.
The wolf pack rejected the lone pup as an *interloper.*

40. Suture [soo-cher]
noun def: a seam as formed in sewing
The *suture* anchors can be made of metal or material that dissolves over time, and do not need to be removed.

41. Subsume [suh b-soom]
verb def: to consider or include an idea, term, proposition
He could *subsume* anything to his phrasing, with his rhythmic hesitations, elisions of words and sudden swells.

42. Perdition [per-dish-uhn]
noun def: complete and utter loss.
Faust brought *perdition* upon himself when he made a deal with the Devil in exchange for power.

43. Incriminate [in-krim-uh-neyt]
verb syn: to accuse of.
He *incriminated* both men to the grand jury.

44. Sepulcher [sep-uh l-kur]
noun def: a tomb; grave; or burial place
The poem that Jessica was reading describes the forgotten *sepulcher* of a valiant knight of the Middle Ages.

45. Stagnant [stag-nuhnt]
adj def: to stop developing. (**)
My mind is *stagnating* from too much TV.

Synonym

1. Foible

    A) Nominal
    B) Weakness
    C) Influential
    D) Distract
    E) Astronomical

2. Harbinger

    A) Pioneer
    B) Edited
    C) Enervate
    D) Captivate
    E) Voluble

3. Fetter

    A) Presumptuous
    B) Reticent
    C) Chain
    D) Penitent
    E) Tenacious

4. Circuitous

    A) Testimony
    B) Persecution
    C) Sponsorship
    D) Sentiment
    E) Roundabout

5. Deviate
>   A) Exploit
>   B) Sojourner
>   C) Benefactor
>   D) Digress
>   E) Protégé

6. Promulgate
>   A) Magnate
>   B) Declare
>   C) Prevaricator
>   D) Raconteur
>   E) Dilettante

7. Perfunctory
>   A) Routine
>   B) Tycoon
>   C) Philanthropist
>   D) Ferocity
>   E) Contentious

8. Foliate
>   A) Gait
>   B) Abreast
>   C) Wrack
>   D) Flourish
>   E) Weaken

Answer keys

1) B 2) A 3) C 4) E 5) D 6) B 7) A 8) D

Antonym

1. Prepossessing
A) Repulsive
B) Indifferent
C) Malignant
D) Precocious
E) Ludicrous

2. Tepid
A) Sinuously
B) Mercilessly
C) Cold
D) Succinctly
E) Rarified

3. Forgo
A) Permeated
B) Continue
C) Illicit
D) Provincial
E) Fabricated

4. Stymie
A) Provocative
B) Sovereign
C) Encroachment
D) Corroborate
E) Encourage

5. Dissension
A) Resurgence
B) Derail
C) Expedite
D) Agree
E) Proliferation

6. Recluse
>A) Belligerent
>B) Slovenly
>C) Extrovert
>D) Fervent
>E) Mollification

7. Atrocious
>A) Inoffensive
>B) Credulity
>C) Reciprocity
>D) Reconciliation
>E) Enmity

8. Subliminal
>A) Immerse
>B) Estrange
>C) Artificial
>D) Adroit
>E) Perception

9. Sumptuous
>A) Sagacious
>B) Frugal
>C) Jocular
>D) Phlegmatic
>E) Apathy

Answer keys

1) A 2) C 3) B 4) E 5) D 6) C 7) A 8) E 9) B

1. **Strenuous** [**stren**-yoo-uhs]
   adj syn: requiring energy.
   > To think deeply is a *strenuous* task.

2. **Titter** [**tit**-er]
   verb def: to laugh in a restrained, self-conscious
   > Some people in the audience *tittered* nervously during an awkward pause in the speech.

3. **Lofty** [**lawf**-tee]
   adj def: arrogantly or condescendingly superior manner.
   > Mary always treats her boyfriend in a *lofty* manner.

4. **Discomfit** [dis-**kuhm**-fit]
   verb syn: to defeat utterly; rout.
   > The army was *discomfited* in every battle.

5. **Inept** [in-**ept**]
   adj syn: without skill; inappropriate. (**)
   > She is *inept* at dealing with people.

6. **Inert** [in-**urt**]
   adj def: not moving; lifeless. (**)
   > In the heat of the desert afternoon, lizards lie *inert*.

7. **Sovereign** [**sov**-er-in]
   adj def: having supreme power.
   > The King did not take kindly to those who refused to recognize his *sovereign* power.

8. **Immolate** [**im**-uh-leyt]
   verb def: to kill as a sacrifice victim, as by fire
   > It was not easy to find out a man who *immolated* himself as an act of protest.

9. **Predilection** [pred-l-**ek**-shuhn]
   noun def: a tendency to think favorably of something.
   > syn: inclination; preference.
   > Jason seemed to have a strong *predilection* for Bach.

10. Preeminent [pree-em-uh-nuhnt]
adj syn: eminent; famous; notable.
> He is *preeminent* in his profession.

11. Omniscience [om-nish-uhns]
noun def: having infinite knowledge.
> Christians believe that because God is *omniscient*, they cannot hide their sins from Him.

12. Lassitude [las-i-tood]
noun syn: indolent; indifference. (*)
> Judy enjoyed the pleasant *lassitude* of the warm summer afternoon.

13. Precarious [pri-kair-ee-uhs]
adj syn: dangerous; perilous. (**)
> Paul enjoys the *precarious* life of an undersea diver.

14. Unkempt [uhn-kempt]
adj syn: disheveled; uncared for. (***)
> Jeremy hated his neighbor's *unkempt* lawn: he thought its neglected appearance had a detrimental effect on neighborhood property value.

15. Susceptible [suh-sep-tuh-buhl]
adj syn: easily influenced; vulnerable.
> Because of her weakened state, Valerie was *susceptible* to infection.

16. Zenith [zee-nith]
noun def: highest point.
> The diva considered her triumphant performance as Carmen with the Metropolitan Opera to be the *zenith* of her career.

17. Lieu [loo]
noun syn: place; stead.
> Martinez gave Tim an IOU in *lieu* of cash.

18. Implicit [im-**plis**-it]
adj def: implied rather than expressly stated.

Tom made an *implicit* agreement with his colleague by nodding his head.

19. Extravagance [ik-**strav**-uh-guhns]
noun syn: excessive; unrestrained.

That sports car is inexcusable *extravagance.*

20. Kindle [**kin**-dl]
verb def: to set fire or ignite; excite or inspire.

With only damp wood to work with, Tilda had great difficulty in *kindling* the campfire.

21. Unparalled [uhn-**par**-uh-leld]
adj syn: unequal; unmatched. (**)

John showed an *unparalled* athletic ability in a football game.

22. Cumbersome [**kuhm**-ber-suhm]
adj syn: burdensome; troublesome; unwieldy; clumsy. (***)

Susan faced unwanted difficulties while dealing with *cumbersome* responsibilities.

23. Rampant [**ram**-puhnt]
adj def: violent in action or spirit; raging; furious.

Paul saw a *rampant* leopard running toward Catherine standing in the middle of the field.

24. Astute [uh-**stoot**]
adj syn: keen penetration; discernment. (**)

The novelist Judy Blumnis an *astute* judgment of human nature; her characters ring true.

25. Amble [**am**-buhl]
verb syn: stroll; saunter.

Jason *ambled* around the town.

26. Conundrum [kuh-**nuhn**-druhm]
noun syn: riddle; puzzle; problem. (**)
> The old man puzzled over the *conundrum* for hours, but eventually gave up in digest.

27. Intact [in-**takt**]
adj syn: not altered; not broken. (***)
> The vase remained *intact* despite rough handling.

28. Beleaguer [bih-**lee**-ger]
verb syn: harass; plague. (*)
> Mickey *beleaguered* her parents to finally give in to her request for a Nintendo.

29. Commensurate [kuh-**men**-sere-it]
adj def: having the same measure; of equal extent or duration.
> Your paycheck should be *commensurated* with the amount of time worked.

30. Ethereal [ih-**theer**-ee-uhl]
adj syn: heavenly; celestial.
> Her delicate, *ethereal* beauty made her a popular model for Pre-Raphaelite artists.

31. Unremitting [uhn-ri-**mit**-ng]
adj def: not remitted as a debt, unpardoned as a sin (**)
> John gave the matter his *unremitting* attention.

32. Gall [gawl]
verb syn: to exasperate and irritate.
> My aunt constantly *galls* my uncle for putting his feet up on the coffee table.

33. Gamely [**geym**-lee]
adverb syn: courageously. (***)
> Though Xena lacked sufficient weapons, she *gamely* faced her opponent.

34. Amorphous [uh-**mawr**-fuh]
adj syn: unclear; doubtful.
> As soon as we have decided on our itinerary, we shall send you a copy; right now, our plans are still *amorphous.*

36. Lien [leen]
noun def: right to possess and sell the property of a debtor.
> The bank took a *lien* on the lender's house to protect themselves in case he defaulted on his loan.

37. Nadir [**ney**-der]
noun def: lowest point. (**)
> As Lou waited in line to audition for the diaper commercial, he realized he had reached the *nadir* of his acting career.

38. Pall [pawl]
verb syn: to loose strength or interest. (***)
> Over time, the model's beauty *palled,* though her haughty attitude remained intact.

39. Quiescent [kwee-**es**-uhnt]
adj syn: inactivity; stillness.
> Bears typically fall into a state of *quiescence* when they hibernate during the winter months.

40. Rectify [**rek**-tuh-fahy]
verb syn: to correct. (*)
> He sent them a check to *rectify* his account.

41. Scintilla [sin-**til**-uh]
noun def: a minute particle; spark.
> This poison is so powerful that a *scintilla* of it is only needed to kill a horse.

42. Testimonial [tes-tuh-**moh**-nee-uh]
noun def: statement testifying to a truth.

The defense lawyers presented many *testimonials* to the good character of the defendant during the trial.

43. Utilitarian [yoo-til-i-**tair**-ee-uhn]
adj syn: efficient; functional; useful.

The suitcase was undeniably *utilitarian,* with its convenient compartments of different sizes, but it was also ugly.

44. Vignette [vin-**yet**]
noun def: decorative design; short literary composition. (**)

The writer's clever little *vignette* was published in a respected literary magazine.

45. Wallow [wol-**oh**]
verb def: to indulge oneself excessively, luxuriate.

Goats *wallowed* in the dust.

" *I just want to take this opportunity to express my most sincere gratitude for all your guidance and assistance in my academic growth and development. I appreciate all you have done to foster my academic excellence. It would have been more difficult to score well on the SAT I without your SAT words book and your tutoring. I will always remember you as I head off to college.* **"**

Joanne *(Ridgewood High School)*
Admitted to University of Illinois at Urbana-Champaign, Education

Synonym

1. Rectify
- A) Encroachment
- B) Amend
- C) Tranquil
- D) Intractable
- E) Dire

2. Pall
- A) Gloom
- B) Convergent
- C) Vanquish
- D) Skeptics
- E) Scorned

3. Interloper
- A) Absence
- B) Lauded
- C) Intermeddler
- D) Bungling
- E) Endorsed

4. Gamely
- A) Tyranny
- B) Deride
- C) Banter
- D) Libel
- E) Brave

5. Beleaguer
A) Controversy
B) Blather
C) Indecisive
D) Harass
E) Arrogant

6. Conundrum
A) Adamant
B) Puzzle
C) Moderate
D) Compatibility
E) Affluence

7. Astute
A) Finesse
B) Recalcitrant
C) Sharp
D) Avant-garde
E) Moribund

8. Scintilla
A) Spark
B) Energetic
C) Plague
D) Concord
E) Linger

Answer keys

1) B 2) A 3) C 4) E 5) D 6) B 7) C 8) A

Antonym

1. Intact
    A) Damaged
    B) Auspicious
    C) Spurious
    D) Munificent
    E) Peeved

2. Cumbersome
    A) Assuaged
    B) Beguiled
    C) Graceful
    D) Nonplussed
    E) Distorted

3. Kindle
    A) Prominent
    B) Subservient
    C) Remorseful
    D) Turn off
    E) Overweening

4. Zenith
    A) Incorruptible
    B) Nadir
    C) Conciliatory
    D) Partisan
    E) Cynical

5. Unkempt
    A) Intricate
    B) Trivial
    C) Stilted
    D) Convoluted
    E) Clean

6. Quiescent
>   A) Candid
>   B) Poignant
>   C) Austere
>   D) Sweeping
>   E) Active

7. Inert
>   A) Mobile
>   B) Tout
>   C) Paramount
>   D) Unprecedented
>   E) Extolled

8. Lofty
>   A) Reprimand
>   B) Apprehensive
>   C) Humble
>   D) Indict
>   E) Mock

9. Inert
>   A) Dehydrate
>   B) Active
>   C) Startle
>   D) Impetuous
>   E) Zenith

Answer keys

1) A 2) C 3) D 4) B 5) E 6) E 7) A 8) C 9) B

* **Abjure**- to reject; abandon formally.
   Abrogate- to put an end to, abolish by authority.

* **Adage**- old saying; proverb; maxim.
   Adamant- uncompromising; unyielding.

* **Adapt**- to accommodate; adjust.
   Adopt- to choose.

* **Aggregate**- collective mass; sum; total.
   Aggrandize- to enlarge; greater in power.

* **Allure**- to entice by charm; attract.
   Allusion- indirect reference.

* **Appropriate** (*adj*)- proper.
   Appropriate (*v*)- to take possession of.

* **Arbitrary**- depending solely on individual will.
   Arbitrate- to mediate; negotiate.
   Articulate- expressed formulated; well spoken.

* **Aver**- to declare to be truth, affirm.
   Avert- to turn away; prevent; hinder.

* **Banish**- to compel to depart, to put away.
   Vanish- to disappear.
   Vanquish- to conquer; overcome.

* **Blight**- to affect; destroy.
   Brazen- bold; shameless; impudent.

* **Callous**- thick-skinned; insensitive.
   Callow- Immature; lacking sophistication.

* **Cessation**- temporary or complete halt.
  Cession- act of giving up something.

* **Circumspect**- cautious; wary.
  Circumvent- to go around; avoid.

* **Cogent**- logically forceful; compelling.
  Cognate- related; similar; akin.

* **Congenial**- similar in taste.
  Congenital- existing since birth.

* **Conjugal**- pertaining to marriage.
  Conjure- to evoke a spirit, cast a spell.

* **Credible**- plausible, believable.
  Credulous- gullible, trusting.

* **Denounce**- to accuse; blame.
  Renounce- to give up
  Denunciation- public condemnation.

* **Deprecate**- to belittle, disparage.
  Depreciate- to loose value gradually.

* **Discrepancy**- difference between
  Discretionary- subject to one's own judgments.

* **Disparage**- to belittle, speak, disrespectful.
  Disparate- dissimilar, different in kind.
  Disparity- contrast, dissimilarity.

* **Doleful**- sad, mournful.
  Dolt- idiot, foolish.
  Doting- excessively fond, loving to excess.

* **Elicit**- to draw out, provoke.
   Implicit- indirect.

* **Eminent**- high in position; repute; prominent
   Imminent- likely to occur at any moment; impending.

* **Empathy**- the intellectual identification with
   Apathy- no feeling
   Sympathy- the harmony of feeling

* **Energize**- to empower; strengthen.
   Enervate- to weaken.

* **Eulogy**- high praise, often in a public speech.
   Euphony- pleasant, harmonious sound.

* **Evict**- to put out or force out
   Evince- to show clearly, display.

* **Exacerbate**- to aggravate, intensify the bad qualities of.
   Exasperate- to irritate.

* **Extol**- to praise.
   Extort- to obtain something by threats.

* **Gall (*noun*)**- bitterness, careless nerve.
   Gall (*verb*)- to exasperate and irritate.

* **Heretical**- opposed to an established religious orthodox.
   Hermetic- tightly sealed.

* **Impassion**- with passion.
   Impassive- showing no emotion.

* **Impertinent**- rude
   Impervious- impossible to penetrate.

* **Implacable**- inflexible; incapable of being pleased.
  Implausible- improbable; inconceivable.

* **Impudent**- arrogant; audacious.
  Impugn- to call into question.

* **Inculcate**- to teach, impress in mind.
  Inculpate- to blame, charge.
  Exculpate- to free from blame.

* **Inept**- clumsy, awkward.
  Inert- not moving; lifeless.

* **Ingenious**- original, clever.
  Ingenuous- straightforward, open; naïve.

* **Ingrate**- ungrateful person
  Ingratiate- to bring oneself purposely into another's good graces.

* **Insidious**- sly, treacherous.
  Invidious- envious; obnoxious.

* **Jaundice**- yellowish discoloration of skin.
  Jaundiced- affected by prejudiced or embittered.

* **Ludicrous**- laughable, ridiculous.
  Lugubrious- sorrowful, mournful.

* **Mendacious**- dishonest.
  Mendicant- beggar.

* **Meretricious**- gaudy; falsely attractive.
  Meritorious- deserving reward or praise.

* **Negligent**- careless; inattentive.
  Negligible- not worth considering.

* **Oblivious**- unaware; inattentive.
   Oblique- indirect; evasive.

* **Ominous**- menacing; threatening.
   Onerous- burdensome.

* **Ordain**- to make someone a priest.
   Ordeal- extremely severe.

* **Pall (*noun*)**- covering that darkens.
   Pall (*verb*)- to loose strengthen or interest.

* **Partisan (*noun*)**- strong supporter.
   Partisan (*adj*)- biased in favor of.

* **Patent (*adj*)**- obvious.
   Patent (*noun*)- official document.

* **Perpetrate**- to commit a crime.
   Perpetuate- to preserve from extinction.

* **Pluck (*verb*)**- to pull strings on a musical instrument.
   Plucky- courageous, spunky.

* **Precarious**- uncertain; tricky; doubtful.
   Vicarious- indirect.

* **Precipitate (*adj*)**- sudden and unexpected.
   Precipitate (*verb*)- to throw down from a height.

* **Preponderous**- majority in member.
   Preposterous- absurd; illogical.

* **Prodigal**- wasteful; extravagant.
   Prodigious- vast; enormous.

* **Propitiate-** to win over, appease.
  Propitious- favorable; advantageous.

* **Ply-** to use diligently.
  Pry- to intrude into; force into.

* **Ravenous-** extremely hungry.
  Ravine- deep, narrow gorge.

* **Scintilla-** trace amount.
  Scintillate- to sparkle, flash.

* **Sloth-** laziness.
  Slovenly- untidy, messy.

* **Solicitous-** concerned; attentive.
  Solicit- to entreat or petition.

* **Speculation-** contemplation act of lacking business risks for financial gain.
  Speculative- involving assumption.

* **Stint (*verb*)-** to be sparing or frugal.
  Stint (*noun*)- period of time spent doing something.

* **Tinge (*verb*)-** to color slightly.
  Tinge (*noun*)- slight amount.

* **Torpid-** lethargic; unable to move.
  Torrid- burning hot; passionate.

* **Tout-** to praise; to extol.
  Taut- to tighten; tense.

* **Turbid-** not clear.
  Turgid- swollen, bloated.

* **Undermine**- to lessen; to weaken
   Underscore- to emphasize; to focus on
   Underlying- Fundamental; Basic

* **Usurp**- to seize by force.
   Usury- practice of lending money at exorbitant rates.

* **Vindicate**- to support a claim.
   Vindictive- spiteful; vengeful.

" *Looking at this book,* Mastering Core SAT Words, *I thought, "Oh, another book on SAT vocabulary," but I immediately changed my thought as soon as I opened the book. I realized how easily this book allowed me to study. All the words were organized. This book, unlike most books on SAT vocabulary, showed me how much to study and what to study. It's a good book if you need something organized!* **"**

Seojung Nam *(Paramus Catholic High School)*

William H. Shin

The primary purpose of this research paper is to find out ways to help high school students improve their SAT Critical Reading/Writing/Essay scores in a formal classroom setting and a given time period. Particularly, this paper will analyze the critical reading/writing questions and the essay topics on the SAT reasoning test. In addition, this paper will also present effective teaching methods, strategies, tactics, and SAT preparation materials, which may have positive effects on high school students who must boost their SAT critical reasoning test scores. Several constructive suggestions, recommendations, findings, and pragmatic strategies will also be provided at the end of this research paper.

The College Board embarked on the SAT (Scholastic Aptitude Test) as the standardized college admission test in 1901, but the meaning of the SAT has since changed. In 1990, the College Board became determined to change the embedded meaning of the Scholastic Aptitude Test into the Scholastic Assessment Test due to the fact that the SAT revealed an inability to effectively and efficiently evaluate the test takers' intellectual academic capabilities. From 1994 through 2004, the name SAT stood alone as a proper noun and was no longer considered an acronym. In 1994, the College Board decided to increase the number of questions from 25 to 40 in regard to the long reading passages, not only to accommodate feasible alterations in future college education, but also to reflect the fundamental change of the educational environment. In addition, an increasing number of studies show that students who have high levels of reading ability in analyzing texts appear to have better chances to succeed in their college academic lives than those who have lower levels of reading ability. Since 2005, the SAT has been known as SAT 1 (the reasoning test) and SAT 2 (the separate subject tests).

Three different sections constitute the SAT Critical Reading Section. Each section consists of sentence completion questions as well as questions that refer to short and long reading passages. The sentence completion questions test the students' abilities to choose the best method to complete a sentence where one or more words have been omitted. In order to improve their test scores, students must have both a high level of reading comprehension and a strong SAT vocabulary. There are several strategies and tactics that can help students find the correct answers in this section.

- First, finding a signal word, such as the phrase *on the contrary*, is crucial for the students to locate the correct answer. The reason is that *on the contrary* sets up a control between a hypothetical change – the change the students might have assumed took place – and the actual change (Green and Wolf, 2007).

- Second, reading the given sentence carefully is another vital factor for the test takers to be able to find the correct answers.

- Third, a great number of case studies show that thinking of a word that makes sense before looking at the answer choices is an effective strategy with which the students can find a word that best completes the sentence's thought (McGraw Hill, 2010). The process is as follows. Before the students look at the answer choices, they try to come up with a word that makes logical sense in this context. Then, they look at the five choices given. If the word the test takers thought of is one of the five choices, they select it as their answer. If the word the test takers thought of is not one of the five choices, they look for a synonym for that word (Noh, Eun Hee and Park, Ki-beom 2009).

- Fourth, using the process of elimination plays a crucial role in helping the students solve the SAT questions. According to the various verbal reports provided by my students, a majority of them have shown that if they are able to eliminate at least two or three of the answer choices, they will find themselves much more comfortable with finding the correct answers.

- Finally, the SAT test takers must familiarize themselves with idiomatic expressions and clichés. In their general tips for answering sentence completion questions, the SAT-makers say, "If an answer is cliché, it may well be right, so do not disregard an answer just because it is a cliché." (Barron's, 2007)

The critical reading questions test students' abilities to understand what they have read by asking questions on content as well as students' reading techniques. Many types of passages are included in this section. One type of passage will be a narrative. These passages are taken from novels, short stories, autobiographies, or personal essays. The second type of passage deals with the sciences, including medicine, botany, zoology, chemistry, physics, and astronomy. The third type of passage is centered on humanities including texts on art, literature, music, philosophy, and folklore. The last type of passage deals with the social sciences, including history, economics, sociology, and government. Some passages may be what the College Board calls argumentative; these passages will present a definite point of view on a subject. One passage will most likely be ethnic in content: Whether it is a historical passage, a personal narrative, or a passage on music, art, or literature, it will deal with concerns of a particular minority group (Barron's 2007).

Five different tactics play a significant role in helping the students to be able to locate the correct answers effectively.

- First, the students should make use of the introductions to acquaint themselves with the text. As a matter of fact, almost every reading passage is preceded by an italicized introduction. As they read the italicized introductory material, they are able to tackle the passage's opening question.

- Second, the students use the line references in the questions to be sure they have gone back to the correct spot in the given passage.

- Third, the students should tackle passages with familiar subjects when they have a choice, for it is extremely difficult for students to continuously concentrate when they read about something that is unfamiliar to them.

- Fourth, when tackling the short passage, the test takers should first read questions that pertain to the reading passage and then read the passage.

- Fifth, in tackling the long passage, the students need to first read the passage, then read the question, for longer passages require a different approach than shorter ones.

The different approaches are as follows:

- Students read as rapidly as possible with understanding, but do not force themselves to fully grasp the content of the passage.

- As students read the opening sentences, they try to anticipate what the passage will be about. They look for whom or what the author is talking about.
- As students continue to read, they will notice sections of the passage in which the author makes major points. This allows students to be able to look for the right section of the text without having to reread the whole passage, even when a question does not point them to a particular line or paragraph. The students should underline key words and phrases in order to keep track of the passage's content.

Finally, the students should familiarize themselves with the major types of reading questions on the test. If the students can recognize just what a given question requires, they will be better able to tell which particular reading tactic to apply. Here are six categories of reading questions the students are sure to face:

- Main Idea - questions that test the student's ability to find the central thought of the passage.

- Specific Detail - questions that test the student's ability to understand what the author states explicitly.

- Inference - questions that test the student's ability to go beyond the author's explicit statement to see what these statements imply.

- Tone/Attitude - questions that test the test taker's ability to sense an author's or character's emotional state.

- Vocabulary-in-Context - questions that test the student's ability to work out the meaning of words from their context. • 6. Technique – questions that test the student's ability to recognize a passage's method of organization or technique (Wolf, 2007).

The Writing section of the SAT is made up of three different kinds of questions: improving sentences, error detection, and improving paragraphs.

Almost half of them are identifying sentence error questions in which the students have to find an error in the underlined section of a sentence; however, the students do not have to correct sentences or explain the errors. The questions in the Writing section test the student's ability to recognize clear, correct, standard written English. In other words, this is the type of writing college professors expect in written papers. Students will be expected to know basic grammar, such as subject-verb agreement, pronoun-antecedent agreement, correct verb tense, correct sentence structure, and correct diction. They will need to know how to recognize a dangling participle and how to spot when two parts of a sentence are clearly connected. They will also need to know when a paragraph is (or is not) properly developed and organized.

There are several test-taking tactics, strategies, and skills that may be able to help students tackle the three different kinds of questions. This paper will also introduce two different SAT test preparation materials, which can benefit those students who are at the beginning or intermediate stage of SAT preparation.

Let us begin with testing tactics associated with identifying sentence errors.

- First, students should use their ear for the language, for they do not have to name the error, or be able to explain why it is wrong. All they have to do is recognize that something is simply wrong.

- Second, students should look first for the most common errors because most sentences will contain some type of error. If students are having trouble in finding mistakes, they should check for some of the common ones: subject-verb agreement, pronoun-antecedent problems, misuse of adjectives and adverbs, and dangling modifiers.

- Third, students must bear in mind that not every sentence will contain an error.

According to the College Board, two to twenty percent of the time, the sentence is correct as it stands. Students should try not to get so caught up in hunting for errors that they start seeing errors that are not there. Students should go with choice E in case no errors strike their eye and the sentence sounds natural to their ear.

Improving sentence questions test students' abilities to spot the form of a sentence that works best. In fact, in these improving sentence questions, students will be presented five different versions of the same sentence. They must be able to choose the best one. The following testing tactics will be conducive for students in finding correct answers.

- First, if students spot an error in the underlined section, they should eliminate any answer choices that repeat the error.

- Second, if students do not spot the error in the underlined section, they should look for changes in the answer choices. When that happens to the students, they should turn to the answer choices and then find the changes in the answer. The changes will tell students what kind of error is being tested.

- Third, students must make sure all parts of the sentence are logically connected, for not all parts of a sentence are created equal. Some parts should be subordinated to the rest, connected with subordinating conjunctions, or relative pronouns.

- Fourth, students must make sure that all parts of a sentence given in a series are similar in form. This tactic is an extremely important tool students should be aware of, since numerous case studies reveal that an increasing number of the SAT Writing questions have been profoundly associated with parallel structure.

- Finally, students must pay particular attention to the shorter answer choices. In fact, this tactic also applies to certain paragraph correction questions. It is a general fact that good prose is normally economical. Often the correct answer choice will be the shortest.

In the improving paragraph questions, the students will confront a flawed student essay followed by six questions. In some cases, students must select the answer choice that best rewrites and combines portions of two separate sentences. In others, students must decide where in the essay a sentence best fits. In still others, students must choose what sort of additional information would most strengthen the writer's argument. There are four different testing tactics that might be able to help students tackle these questions successfully.

- First, the students should first read the passage, then read the questions. This tactic leads the students to a reasonable idea of what the student author is trying to say before they set out to correct the rough first draft.

- Second, students should first tackle questions that ask them to improve individual sentences, then tackle the ones that ask them to strengthen the passage as a whole. In the sentence correction questions, students have just been eliminating ineffective sentences and selecting effective ones. It generally takes less time to spot an effective sentence than it does to figure out a way to strengthen an argument or link two paragraphs. It is worth noting that the process of elimination can be applied to any questions on the SAT.

- Third, students consider whether the addition of transition signals – words or phrases – would strengthen the passage or particular sentences within it. If the essay is trying to contrast two ideas, the essay might benefit from the addition of a contrast signal. If one portion of the essay is trying to support or continue a thought developed elsewhere in the passage, the essay might benefit from the addition of a support signal. If the essay is trying to indicate that one thing causes another, the essay might benefit from the addition of a cause and effect signal.

- Fourth, students must go back to the passage to verify each answer choice when they tackle the questions. Students should see whether their revised version of a particular sentence sounds right in its context. In addition, students must ask themselves whether their choice follows naturally from the previous sentence.

Finally, some errors are more common than others in this section. Here are the errors that appear frequently on the SAT:

- run-on sentences
- sentence fragment
- errors in the case of a noun or pronoun
- errors in subject-verb agreement
- errors in pronoun-number agreement
- errors in the tense or form of a verb
- errors in logical comparison
- adjective and adverb confusion
- errors in modification and word order
- errors in parallelism
- errors in diction or idiom
- wordiness and redundancies.

Students must study these common errors and memorize them. It is important to note that students should continue to study these errors until they are able to identify the common errors when they complete practice exercises as well as the actual SAT. Two reference books, *Rules of the Game* (by Mary Page, Peter Guthrie, and Sloan Sable, published by Educators Publishing Service) and *McGraw-Hill's SAT, 2010 Edition* provide not only detailed and sufficient explanations about errors and grammar rules related to questions found on the SAT, but also offer a variety of drills through which students can improve their scores on the SAT Writing section.

This section explains the basic guidelines for writing an essay on the SAT and will include tactics that test takers can use when dealing with unfamiliar essay topics. In addition, the section will acquaint test takers with a host of resources that will help them develop their essay-writing skills. In the past, the Educational Testing Service (ETS) has used three types of essay questions on the SAT Writing Test. The College Board uses a similar formula for the current SAT writing prompts.

There are several tactics and strategies that may help students not only enhance their writing skills but also improve their essay scores. First, students should familiarize themselves with the most common types of essay questions. The first type of essay question asks students to respond to a statement. The second asks students to choose between contrasting statements. The third type of prompt asks students to complete a statement. Although the three question types may appear on the surface to be different, they have much in common. Each question demands that the students take a stance and provide evidence to support that stance. Not only must test takers argue a point, but they must also have content that is of quality in order to receive high scores. Students will only deal with three different aforementioned topics. According to the administrators of the College Board, essay graders, who are high school teachers and college professors, will be looking for whether or not a student's subject matter is related to the given topic, whether a student's stance is insightful, and whether the stance is persuasive. Students should take a firm stance in their essays and stick to it. In order to receive a score between 10 and 12, students must go beyond their personal experiences. They must make their essays more interesting and be sure to incorporate meaningful connections. Although graders will look at grammar and punctuation as a part of a successful essay, the errors in this area will not have a detrimental influence on the students' overall scores. In other words, students can get high scores with a few grammar mistakes. So, test takers do not have to be seriously concerned with grammar or punctuation mistakes. Further, students' essays must be legible, for the graders expect an organized and readable piece of writing that makes an argument supported by real examples. Students must also be sure to use specific examples in their arguments. Students need to cite evidence to support their examples, for arguing their point of view without having specific reasons is not convincing and will not receive high essay scores.

Finally, the length of student essays has a considerable impact on their overall writing score. If a student wants to receive an essay score ranging from 10-12, he/she must write 300-400 words in a well-written essay. Students can self-grade their essays by following these criteria:

- The essay has a clear sentence on the given issue.
- The essay provides specific supporting examples and evidence.
- The essay has logical organization.
- The essay uses appropriate transitions between ideas.
- The essay uses various sentence structures and words.
- The sentences in the essay are clear and have an even tone.

As a matter of fact, I have been teaching the SAT Critical Reading and Writing Section for the past twelve years in several private institutions located in both Palisades Park, New Jersey and Manhattan. In order to meet the demands of the students who have taken my SAT class, I have spent numerous hours, along with my colleagues, gathering a multiplicity of information related to the SAT questions and analyzing recently released questions by the College Board. These efforts have led me to realize that there are no absolutely impeccable strategies, tactics, or teaching methods that can perfectly satisfy my students' relentless demands; however, through ongoing investigation and research I have discovered several interesting results that students need to be aware of in order to prepare for the SAT more effectively.

- First, the passages vary in length and are taken from a variety of fields, not revising the original texts.

- Second, the critical reading items measure a test taker's literal and inferential comprehension ability, and the writing items focus mainly on a student's vocabulary and grammar proficiency.

- Third, the questions are stereotyped, repetitive, and simple; therefore, a majority of students are accustomed to these types of questions and are able to easily understand them.

- Fourth, passage difficulty is appropriate for high school students, but the item difficulty is low for them. Because all items are selected from the Item Bank according to item difficulty, the SAT can constantly maintain the degree of difficulty.

- Fifth, the essay section tests students' abilities to articulate a coherent argument, supporting a point of view on an issue specified on the test.

- Finally, the SAT reasoning test assesses the critical thinking skills the students need for academic success in college.

I would like to conclude this study with the fact that I am grateful to my SAT students who have helped me gather the information needed in order to complete this study. I am also deeply indebted to those who have encouraged me to continue to work as an SAT instructor. Most important, they inspired me to realize that pursuing higher education is necessary for me to meet the education philosophy that I firmly believe in. I would like to dedicate this study to them.

Camara, W. J. & Echterncht, G. (2000), The SAT 1 and High School Grades: Utility in predicting Success in College, Research Notes, RN-10, The College Board.

Cech, S.J. (2007), College-Admissions Group Weighs Call to Dump SAT, Education Week, 27 (6), pp.8-9.

Geiser, S. & Studley R. (2002), UC and the SAT: Predictive Validity and Differential Impact of SAT 1 and SAT 2 at the University of California, Educational Assessment, 8 (1), pp.1-26.

Green, H. & Green, M.(2007), Admissions trends to Watch 2007-2008, (www.universitybusiness.com).

Honawar, V. (2005), Colleges Hesitate to Embrace SAT Writing Test, Education Week, 24 (39), pp.-1-5.

Katz, S. & Lautenschlager, G. (2001), The Contribution of Passage and No-passage Factors to Item Performance on the SAT Reading Task, Educational Assessment, 7 (2), pp.-165-176.

Lawrence, I. M. Rigol, G. W. Essen, T. V. & Jackson, C. A. (2003), A Historical Perspective on the Content of the SAT, College Board Report No. 2003-3, ETS RR-03-10, College Entrance Examination Board.

The College Board (2006), The Official SAT Study Guide, New York: The College Board.

The College Board (2007). SAT Subject tests preparation booklet 2007-2008, New York: The College Board

Wayne J. Camara & Gary Echternacht (2000), *The SAT 1 and High School Grades: Utility in Predicting Success in College,* Research Notes, RN-10, The College Board.

" I have always struggled with the vocabulary on the SAT. There were just so many words to study from. After getting William Shin's Mastering Core SAT Words, *I knew exactly what to study. The book consists of 1395 vocabulary words selected right from the real SAT tests. This book has helped me improve my vocabulary tremendously. If you're having any trouble on the Critical Reading section of the SAT test, I highly recommend that you get this book.* **"**

Bonkyu Ku *(Arlington High School)*

CPSIA information can be obtained
at www.ICGtesting.com
Printed in the USA
FFOW01n2053040615
13957FF